W9-BIJ-838

CORBIN BLEU
TO THE LIMIT

An Unauthorized Biography by Betsy West

PRICE STERN SLOAN
Published by the Penguin Group
Penguin Group (USA) Inc., 375 Hudson Street,
New York, New York 10014, U.S.A.
Penguin Group (Canada), 90 Eglinton Avenue East, Suite 700,
Toronto, Ontario, Canada M4P 2Y3
(a division of Pearson Penguin Canada Inc.)
Penguin Books Ltd, 80 Strand, London WC2R 0RL, England
Penguin Ireland, 25 St Stephens Green, Dublin 2, Ireland
(a division of Penguin Books Ltd)
Penguin Group (Australia), 250 Camberwell Road,
Camberwell, Victoria 3124, Australia
(a division of Pearson Australia Group Pty Ltd)
Penguin Books India Pvt Ltd, 11 Community Centre,
Panchsheel Park, New Delhi - 110 017, India
Penguin Group (NZ), Cnr Airborne and Rosedale Roads,
Albany, Auckland 1310, New Zealand
(a division of Pearson New Zealand Ltd)
Penguin Books (South Africa) (Pty) Ltd, 24 Sturdee Avenue,
Rosebank, Johannesburg 2196, South Africa

Penguin Books Ltd, Registered Offices:
80 Strand, London WC2R 0RL, England

Photo credits: Cover: courtesy of Michael Bezjilan/WireImage.com; Insert photos: First page
courtesy of Howard Wise/Shooting Star; second page courtesy of David Gabber/Photorazzi,
Michael Bezjilan/WireImage.com; third page courtesy of C. Caraballo/WireImage.com,
J. Sciulli/WireImage.com; fourth page courtesy of David Dowling/Shooting Star.

Library of Congress Cataloging-in-Publication Data

West, Betsy.
Corbin Bleu : to the limit : an unauthorized biography / by Betsy West.
p. cm.
ISBN 978-0-8431-2685-3 (pbk.)
1. Bleu, Corbin, 1989– —Juvenile literature. 2. Actors—United States—Biography—Juvenile
literature. I. Title.
PN2287.B457W47 2007
791.4302'8092—dc22
[B]
2006101846

10 9 8 7 6 5 4 3

CORBIN BLEU
TO THE LIMIT

An Unauthorized Biography by Betsy West

PSS!
PRICE STERN SLOAN

Contents

Introduction

Corbin Bleu, Breakout Star!

Corbin Bleu isn't just another flash-in-the-pan young star, famous one minute and unheard of the next. Ever since he was a kid, crazy-haired Corbin's been following in his father's footsteps, using his terrific talents in every way possible. He's already proven his acting chops in movies like the Disney Channel's hit *High School Musical* and *Catch That Kid*, and the Discovery Kids show *Flight 29 Down*.

Next up? More acting, of course, including the sequel to *High School Musical* and *Jump In!*—but that's not all for this multitalented guy. His new album, *Another Side*, will debut in April 2007. The album will showcase the young singer as a surefire heir to the Justin Timberlake throne, mixing R&B and pop flavors on top of great beats.

So what is it that makes Corbin so different from all those other guys (besides his trademark crazy-curly hair)? Well, he's worked really hard to get where he is, and he's spent his whole life doing it. This soulful, funny, and kind young star really is taking it to the limit—and luckily for us, he's not stopping anytime soon.

Chapter 1

Corbin 101: All the Corbin Essentials

Think you know everything about Corbin Bleu? Even if you've seen every single movie, watched every show, and even downloaded sneak peeks of his upcoming videos from YouTube, we bet at least one thing on this list will surprise you.

1. Name: Corbin Bleu—born Corbin Bleu Reivers

2. Nickname: Bleuman

3. Birthday: February 21, 1989

4. Birthplace: Brooklyn, New York

5. Height: 5'9"

6. Eyes: Brown

7. Current home: Los Angeles, California

8. Zodiac sign: Corbin is a Pisces. (We'll explain more later!)

9. Parents: Martha and David

10. Siblings: Corbin's the oldest of four kids. He has three younger sisters—Hunter, Phoenix, and Jag. Hunter and Phoenix are actors, too.

11. Famous relatives: Both of Corbin's parents are actors. His father, David Reivers, is best known for his role in the movie *Poseidon*, but he's also been in tons of TV shows—everything from *The Gilmore Girls* to *Charmed* to *Home Improvement*. He'll also be in Corbin's next movie, *Jump In!*—playing Corbin's dad! When the casting was announced, Corbin wrote in his online journal at corbinbleu.com, "My dad is one of the people that I have always dreamed of working with and now I finally have the opportunity to." And

when filming was complete, he wrote, "Working with my dad was definitely one of the highlights of my career thus far."

12. Can't start the day without: Pancakes and a chai latte from Coffee Bean

13. Favorite school subject: Corbin is tutored on the set of whichever project he's working on, so he's never gotten the typical high-school experience. But he loves math and science!

14. Favorite book: Corbin reads a lot—everything from psychology textbooks to classic novels.

15. Favorite food: Corbin's an all-American guy. His favorite meal is a burger and french fries.

16. Favorite musician: Prince is Corbin's all-time favorite musician—he even saw one of Prince's shows once, which he thought was great. He also loves eighties music. And his favorite rapper is Kanye West.

17. Favorite TV show: Corbin loves *The Amazing Race*, but he's also a huge fan of *Futurama*.

18. Favorite sport: Basketball! Well, sort of. He learned how to play the game for *High School Musical*, and he told *Scholastic News* that he struggled with it at first. Corbin said, "I was really happy when we switched to dance" for other parts of the movie, because dancing has always been his favorite thing to do—he's danced since he was a little kid! In *High School Musical*, he was able to combine both basketball and dance for "Get'cha Head in the Game," one of the big performance pieces in the movie.

19. Goal for the future: Corbin loves performing, but he'd like to perform some of the magic behind the scenes, too. He told *Time for Kids* that his goal is to become a producer. "I want to be able to control and have power over my own projects. I want to put together my own movie!" he said.

20. Hero: Corbin has a lot of respect for Denzel Washington —not only for the Hollywood star's skills, but because

Denzel's an African-American who's really made it to the big-time. (One day, Corbin would love to produce a movie starring Denzel!) Corbin also admires Johnny Depp. And of course he looks up to his dad!

21. Secret talent: It might not be much of a secret that Corbin's an amazing tap dancer!

22. Pets? None. Corbin told teenmusic.com, "A house of six is crazy enough as it is!"

23. Favorite movie: It changes all the time, but he loves *Chicago* and *The Rocky Horror Picture Show*. Both movies combine dance, music, and acting—so it's no surprise they're Corbin's faves!

24. Lucky charm: Corbin has the bottom of a tap shoe attached to his keychain to remind him of his favorite thing—dancing.

25. Weirdest thing in his house: A leopard-print toilet seat!

Chapter 2

Anything But Average

Corbin Bleu has been working for a very, very long time—since he was practically a baby! At the incredibly young age of two, Corbin began his career by appearing in commercials on television for products like Life cereal and Bounty. He was signed as a professional model when he was only four. And by 1996, he had a small guest role on *ER*. How many other seven-year-old kids can say they've been on a show with George Clooney?

But Corbin's never let his early rise to fame go to his head. He's a normal guy who loves hanging out with his friends, watching movies, playing games with his sisters, and going to school. He still lives with his family—no underage clubbing and tabloid stories for this guy. Sure, he's quite a bit more famous than most seventeen-year-olds, but that hasn't stopped him from living a normal life.

Of course, when you're a Disney star, a normal life isn't exactly normal! Other teens might dream about a vacation in Hawaii, and some lucky ones get to go to the island paradise for a few days. To shoot the first season of *Flight 29 Down*, Corbin got to actually live in Hawaii for three months! Sometimes his mom or dad stayed with him; other times, he was joined by his aunt and uncle. Corbin and the rest of the cast lived in a huge condo a few blocks from the beach.

That was an incredible experience for him. He told timeforkids.com, "It was absolutely amazing! Hawaii is a really beautiful and relaxing place. We had the beach. We had the stars at night."

However wonderful Corbin's experiences as a professional actor have been, it isn't all fun and games. He told timeforkids.com that one of the hardest things about his job is having to be away from his family, especially his three little sisters. "Everything has its ups and downs," he said, proving that not only does he have talent, but he's also got his head firmly on his shoulders.

It's not all limos and red-carpet premieres for Corbin. His downtime is really important to him. And it turns out that his favorite interests are exactly what you'd expect to hear from a teenage guy. He obviously loves to dance, sing, and act. But he also loves to go bowling, ice-skating, and to go to shows with his friends. And when there's nothing to do, he often has his friends over to watch movies at his house.

One of the only differences between Corbin and any other teenager is that he isn't crazy about video games. He's just found other things to do with his time—like playing basketball! It turns out that the basketball phenom you see on *High School Musical* barely knew the difference between dribbling and shooting when he began working on the film.

Of course, he had to learn how to play in order to portray basketball jock Chad Danforth, and Corbin's the kind of actor who doesn't just act. He learned how to play ball, and now he can even spin a basketball on his finger—not bad, for someone who's been playing for only a year or two!

It's that kind of versatility that really makes an actor, and luckily, Corbin was among a group of friends while shooting *High School Musical*—he was able to relax and learn the moves he needed to learn.

And in turn, during the numerous dance numbers,

his acting chops made way for his many dance skills. He told *Scholastic News* online, "I was so happy when we switched to dance because it was sort of the opposite. I have been dancing since I was two years old. Dance is my comfort zone. That is what I was very comfortable with and some of the actors have never danced before. It was sort of a little switch there."

Corbin has been able to learn a lot as an actor, and not just things you can learn in a class. Though he's never taken acting classes, he did study theater at the Los Angeles County High School for the Arts, a prestigious high school in Los Angeles, California, that has curriculum in dance, music, theater, and visual arts. But much of what he's learned has taken place on the sets of his TV shows and films.

To film *Jump In!*, Corbin had to familiarize himself with two unfamiliar sports—boxing and jumping rope. He got into the best shape of his life for the movie.

Not all of his new skills are athletic, though. Corbin stars on the show *Flight 29 Down*, which is a survival show about a group of teenagers who find themselves stranded on an island when their plane crashes. Due to filming this show in Hawaii, Corbin says he feels much better prepared to survive if he were ever in a situation like that.

He told *Scholastic News* online, "You never know when something like this can happen. I mean, I got to learn how to start a fire using sticks. We learn so many different things about survival: I learned to climb a coconut tree and how to crack open a coconut, which is extremely hard." That's not something most kids learn in high school!

In high school, a lot of people are starting to think about dating and romance. Even though the only romantic act in *High School Musical* was a sweet, innocent kiss on the cheek, Corbin has a love life and is definitely interested in the ladies. In a live chat on teenmusic.com, Corbin said, "I really like girls that are outgoing, that have lots of energy. Sweet, smart, funny, and pretty, of course!"

He doesn't currently have a girlfriend, but he does like to date. He loves girls who are thoughtful and easy to talk to. However, it's really important to him that his date is a down-to-earth person, too. He's not into boy-crazy fans; he would rather start off slow, as friends, and gradually get to know a person.

Unlike some of his peers, this guy would take a relationship seriously. The most important thing he looks for in a relationship is honesty. It is incredibly important to him to be able to tell his girlfriend everything—and he absolutely expects the same in return. Maybe that's why he has been taking it slow when it comes to relationships—to find someone trustworthy, it's important to take your time!

Corbin told *Teen Magazine* online, "I think the most important part of a relationship is having an open relationship, being able to talk to each other about everything. If there's something that is bothering you about me or anything that is going on between us that doesn't seem right, let's not let it go and hope that it will repair itself, because that might just make it worse, and it will continue and could ruin the relationship. I think [the most important thing is] being able to understand that you can come up to me and talk to me about anything. Honesty."

Of course, Corbin does have celebrity crushes! Like a lot of guys Corbin's age, he thinks Angelina Jolie is number one on that list. He also likes Jennifer Garner, the star of TV's *Alias* and the movie *13 Going on Thirty*. One of his dreams is to make a movie with Angelina. But so far, his best working experience has been with the cast of *Flight 29 Down*.

In a live chat on teenmusic.com, he said, "I'm a very outgoing person. I'm always happy. I'm one of those people who are always smiling. If somebody described me to somebody else, they'd say the kid with the curly hair with the big smile on his face. I get along with everybody."

He's lucky to be really close with the actors he works with on *Flight 29 Down*. The actors lived in a Hawaiian condo for three months. Though they each had their own rooms, living in such close quarters meant they all got to know one another really well. He told chatters on teenmusic.com that the *Flight 29 Down* cast is "Probably the closest cast possible. The second we met we all became great friends. We still hang out. We hang out on the island when we're shooting in Hawaii, we hang out here in LA."

Corbin loves being on a set and hanging out with his fellow cast members. And his fellow cast members love him, too!

Lucas Grabeel, who played Ryan Evans on *High*

School Musical, told teenhollywood.com that the cast of *High School Musical* got along really well. He said, "We had two weeks of basically hang-out time and bonding time while we were doing our dance rehearsals. You know, rigorous rehearsals all day long, and you're kind of taking a water break or whatever and just hanging out, which was a great chance to connect and gel with everybody before we actually had a camera on us starting to film things. So by the time we started to shoot, we knew each other pretty well."

Another cast member, Zac Efron, who starred as Troy Bolton in *High School Musical*, agreed. He told teenhollywood.com, "We were very close. We all hung out every day after filming. We'd go out to dinner or movies. We had fun. We're all very tight still to this day."

So Corbin's got a normal love life, a normal family, and normal friendships. But his life does have its differences. Specifically, his fame has started to rise, and that's changing things for him. Craziest moment of fame? A girl once asked him to autograph her stomach!

He told teenmusic.com, "I'm not to that point yet where I would get mobbed. Most of the time I'm usually with my family. If there is a fan that comes by they'll just ask me for my autograph. But it doesn't happen too often." While he hasn't had too hard of a time going out in public and getting mobbed by adoring fans, projects on the horizon may very well rocket Corbin into an entirely new sphere of fame.

Still, Corbin wouldn't change a thing—in fact, while he plans on going to college to study psychology, he doesn't think he'll ever stop acting. And since he's been working since he was two, it's in his blood.

So while Corbin Bleu might seem like a normal kid who happens to have a really exciting life, we think he's pretty extraordinary!

Chapter 3

A New York State of Mind

Corbin Bleu Reivers was born February 21, 1989, to parents Martha and David Reivers. He was born in Brooklyn, which is one of the five boroughs of New York City.

Vibrant, colorful New York was the perfect place for someone like Corbin to grow up. There are tons of Broadway shows, concerts, dance performances, and artistic shows every single day. With two actor parents, Corbin must have been exposed to all the theatrical experiences New York has to offer. With just a ride on the subway or a quick trip in a taxi, little Corbin could be in Manhattan, taking in the sights and watching art and music happen right in front of him.

New York is also a very multicultural city. Corbin's dad is Jamaican-American, and his mother is Italian-American. In his online journal at corbinbleu.com, Corbin wrote that his heritage is "a spicy blend."

That kind of cultural richness in Corbin's life has been both a source of pride and, sometimes, of stress. He has struggled with being a mixed-race kid, especially with casting agents. Sometimes they think he's too Jamaican-looking; sometimes they think he's too Caucasian.

Corbin told *The Star Scoop*, "A lot of times, they're not looking for your type, especially because I'm mixed. A lot of times they either want to go full-on Caucasian or they want to go full-on black. They either want somebody who is really black and from the street, and urban, and a little bit ghetto, or they want a Caucasian. That's probably one of the hardest struggles for me. You never know when work is going to come in."

But in New York, with people from every background, country, religion, and race imaginable, Corbin and his family fit right in.

Corbin still loves New York, even though his family is now based in Los Angeles, California. Christmastime, especially, is amazing for him in New York—the lights, the tree at Rockefeller Center, and the window displays in the big department stores all make New York City a winter wonderland during the holiday season.

Christmas is Corbin's favorite holiday, and, as he

told *Family Screen Scene*, "Especially in New York. It's magical."

He has also said that one of the most romantic dates he could imagine would take place while ice-skating, and what better time than during the holiday season, skating at the famous rink in Rockefeller Center or in Central Park?

When Corbin was seven, his family moved to Los Angeles, but by then, Corbin had been working for quite a few years. At the age of two, Corbin began doing modeling work. He started out doing print work, modeling in catalogs and advertisements in magazines. He also began learning to dance.

Part of the reason Corbin began working so early was that both of his parents are actors. They've both helped him a lot.

Corbin told *The Star Scoop*, "I have really great parents who have constantly kept me grounded my whole life." Having a close-knit family has instilled a sense of self-confidence in Corbin, which has in turn impacted his acting career. Being that comfortable with oneself doesn't come easily, but a warm, loving family helps.

Of course, while Corbin's parents kept him

grounded and laid-back, they also helped him with his early career. Their support has meant a lot to Corbin, and he knows he owes much of his success to his mom and dad.

Corbin's mom, Martha, attended the famous New York City High School of Performing Arts, where she met Corbin's dad.

That high school was the inspiration for the 1980 movie *Fame*, which *Entertainment Weekly* called one of the best high-school movies ever made. Some of the high school's well-known alumni include *Friends* star Jennifer Aniston, movie star Wesley Snipes, and *Buffy the Vampire Slayer*'s Sarah Michelle Gellar—among many, many other dancers, entertainers, musicians, and artists.

Corbin's dad, David, has been in tons of television shows and movies. Corbin has said that his dad is one of his most important heroes. When Corbin was young, he'd watch his dad perform, and that was a huge inspiration for him. Corbin told the *Honolulu Advertiser* that his dad "was right beside me, coaching me, my entire life."

Having parents who were familiar with the industry was helpful to Corbin, especially when he was a little kid. Some kids might be traumatized if they tried out for a role or auditioned for a modeling job and didn't get it. But Corbin was taught from an early age that he shouldn't take it personally if he wasn't chosen.

He told *Scholastic News*, "That was something that my parents explained to me when I was young. Also, since I started when I was two, I had become so used to it by [the time I was] six or seven. One of the best parts about having started so early was knowing what would happen in an audition, and that if I did not get it, it would not be a big deal."

Okay, so maybe he didn't get the job every single time he went in for an audition. But from a very young age, Corbin was doing something right. By the time he was four, he had a contract with the legendary Ford Modeling Agency.

The Ford Modeling Agency was founded by Eileen and Jerry Ford in 1946 as an agency to represent models. The agency has also represented Corbin's *High School Musical* costar Ashley Tisdale, as well as tons of other famous actors, models, and other celebrities. The list of past and present clients reads like a who's who of famous people, including everyone from famous fashion icon Twiggy to ex-*OC* star Mischa Barton to Kirsten Dunst and Lindsay Lohan. And in 1991, the list grew to include Corbin Bleu.

Soon, Corbin was in ads for the Gap, Macy's, Target, Toys "Я" Us, and more. He modeled clothes in *Parenting*, *Child*, and *American Baby* magazines. His face was even on some toy and game packaging. Can you imagine seeing yourself on the box of a new board game? Corbin did!

Corbin's first professional theatrical performance was when he was six years old. He performed as a homeless kid in the off-Broadway play *Tiny Tim Is Dead*. That experience was important for Corbin. He has always felt like the theater is in his blood, and his part in *Tiny Tim Is Dead* was his first major role.

It wasn't an easy role, either. *Tiny Tim Is Dead*, written by Barbara Lebow, is a play about a group of homeless people, and Corbin's character is an abandoned child who is also mute. That's pretty heavy stuff for a six-year-old.

And Corbin was the only kid in the play. He and five adults portrayed homeless people on Christmas Eve who decide to put together their own production of the famous Charles Dickens story *A Christmas Carol*. The play's author worked with many homeless groups, and the play is about the sad and often hopeless plight of the homeless.

Clearly, because of his acting career, parts of Corbin's early life were anything but average. Not many kids have to think about what it might be like to be homeless, or have a disability, unless they're personally impacted by someone in those situations.

However, in a lot of ways, Corbin did have a normal childhood—as normal as is possible when you're on your way to becoming famous, anyway. He got a lot of love from his parents, and he adores his three younger sisters. His family matters to him, and he's a source of pride for both of his parents.

Corbin's mom told the *Honolulu Advertiser*, "He has his head screwed on right. He knows what he wants and has a great work ethic."

And soon after Corbin's role in *Tiny Tim Is Dead*, Corbin and his family were ready to continue Corbin's work, and to make a big change in their lives, too.

They packed up and headed west to California!

Chapter 4

Go West, Young Star!

I n California, it was time for seven-year-old Corbin to focus on his career. After all, he'd already been working for five years!

Corbin's first recurring role was in the ABC network's television show *High Incident*, a crime drama created by Steven Spielberg, the director who's famous for filming *E.T.* Because it was on at the same time as the incredibly popular sitcom *Friends*, *High Incident* was on the air for only two seasons, but it was enough for Hollywood to sit up and take notice of young Corbin.

Another of his early projects was a guest spot on *ER* in 1996. *ER* was one of the most popular TV shows ever, and Corbin acted alongside George Clooney, the two-time winner of *People Magazine*'s Sexiest Man of the Year.

George was on *ER* between 1994 and 1999, and later went on to star in movies like *Batman & Robin*,

Ocean's 11, and *Good Night and Good Luck*. He also had a recurring role on the sitcom *Roseanne* during the late 1980s and early 1990s.

George Clooney is mega-famous, and it was a thrill for little Corbin to shoot scenes with him. Perhaps George is still an inspiration to Corbin—George has executive-produced tons of hit movies, and since producing is a goal Corbin has, it's likely that he has followed George's career and looked up to the older actor.

In 1997, when Corbin was only eight years old, he got his first role in a feature film. *Soldier*, directed by Paul W.S. Anderson, starred Kurt Russell. The movie was a futuristic science-fiction flick. In it, humans are raised only to be part of a huge military. Corbin played a little boy named Johnny.

In a live chat on teenmusic.com, Corbin told his fans, "That was my first big movie. You couldn't even tell it was me, though, because my head was shaved!"

Though his role in *Soldier* wasn't a huge part, the movie quickly piqued Corbin's interest in performing in more films.

The rush and thrill of acting in major movies got to him, and it wasn't long before he had another role, in the 1998 surfing flick *Board Heads*, which was written and directed by John Quinn.

That movie was quickly followed by *Family Tree* in 1999, which won a Director's Gold Award at the Santa Clarita International Film Festival and a Special Jury Award at WorldFest Houston for the best independent theatrical feature film in the family and children category.

Family Tree also starred Naomi Judd, who was part of the hit musical group The Judds with her daughter. And other cast members included real-life brothers Andrew and Matthew Lawrence.

It must have been fun for Corbin to be around Andy and Matt, who were used to the acting life, too— and what's more, the Lawrences were used to being part of an acting family. Their big brother, Joey, starred in the hit 1990s show *Blossom* for five years, and has gone on to star in tons of TV shows and movies. For his part, Joey performed the theme song to *Family Tree*. And unbelievably, while all this acting was going on, Corbin was admitted to an all-star high school, the Los Angeles School of the Performing Arts. He also studied with the famous dancer Debbie Allen at the Debbie Allen Dance

Academy in Los Angeles. Debbie Allen's first famous role was in the movie *Fame* in 1980, in which she played Lydia Grant. She also was in the TV version of the movie, which ran for five years in the 1980s. (She's also the sister of Phylicia Rashad, who is most famous for playing Clair Huxtable on *The Cosby Show*.) Debbie produced the Cosby spin-off *A Different World* for six seasons on NBC, and has also won two Tony Awards. She was in a number of Broadway shows, as well. Debbie also directed several episodes of *Raven*, *All of Us*, and *Family Ties*.

Corbin was a very busy young actor. After *Family Tree*, he went on to play Butch in *Mystery Men* in 1999, which the *New York Times* called a "crafty, tongue-in-cheek satire."

The movie, about a bunch of self-styled superheroes, got good reviews. *Variety*, the insider's guide to all things Hollywood, said that *Mystery Men* was "sharply written, with a lavish look and top-drawer effects adding to the appeal of its large and talented cast." And our Corbin was part of that group at the young age of ten!

Mystery Men was based on a comic-book series published by Dark Horse Publishing. Starring Ben Stiller,

Janeane Garofalo, Hank Azaria, and William H. Macy, the movie was packed with comedic talent, and some people compared it to *Austin Powers*, which had recently been a blockbuster.

While filming *Mystery Men*, Corbin had the chance to work with some of the most respected comedians and actors in the business. Corbin played Butch, the ten-year-old son of the Shoveler, a struggling superhero who was portrayed by William H. Macy. Butch was one of the Shoveler's five kids, and Corbin definitely had some hilarious lines in the movie.

It must have been exciting for Corbin to work with William H. Macy. He has been nominated for Oscars, won Emmys, and has been in dozens of movies like *Fargo*, *Jurassic Park III*, and *Pleasantville*.

Other notable stars in *Mystery Men* were funny lady Janeane Garofalo, who's been in *The Truth About Cats and Dogs* and *Reality Bites*, and Ben Stiller, whose recent films *Zoolander* and *Meet the Fockers* have done incredibly well in the box office.

After the success of *Mystery Men*, Corbin was off to another cult favorite movie, 1999's *Galaxy Quest*. *Galaxy Quest*, directed by Dean Parisot and written by

David Howard and Robert Gordon, is a movie about the cast of a canceled sci-fi show that has to save Earth when aliens attack. It's a spoof on *Star Trek*–like shows, and many of its fans loved it for its satirical look at science-fiction TV.

Galaxy Quest was well reviewed; the *New York Times* wrote, "Whether you love *Star Trek* or laugh at it, your starship is about to come in, docking in the form of *Galaxy Quest*, an amiable comedy that simultaneously manages to spoof these popular futuristic space adventures and replicate the very elements that have made them so durable. . . . In the parched comic landscape that now stretches over much of planet Earth, *Galaxy Quest* may not be a monument to the genre, but it offers a ray of hope for the future."

Corbin played young Tommy Webber, the child version of Daryl Mitchell's grown-up Tommy Webber character in the movie.

Other actors in the film included Tim Allen, who's most famous for his role on *Home Improvement*; *Veronica Mars*'s Enrico Colantoni; Sigourney Weaver, who starred in the *Alien* movies; and Tony Shaloub, who stars in USA Network's *Monk*. Again, Corbin's character got some great lines in the movie, but the most important thing for him was the experience of acting in another major film with some pretty serious stars!

Tim Allen is probably most famous for his role on the 1991–1999 show *Home Improvement*, and he's also starred in the *Santa Clause* movies, among many, many others. He was nominated for two Emmy Awards for *Home Improvement*, and was nominated five times for a Golden Globe Award, winning one in 1995. He also won the Nickelodeon Blimp Award in 1994, 1995, 1996, and 1997 for the favorite actor in a TV show. As a true child of the 1990s, Corbin must have been thrilled to work with Tim Allen!

The movie was not only well reviewed, but it was also award-winning. Tim Allen won a Saturn Award from the Academy of Science Fiction, Fantasy, and Horror Movies, and the film was nominated for eight other Saturn Awards. And both Tim Allen and Sigourney Weaver were nominated for favorite actor awards from Blockbuster Entertainment.

The movie won a Hugo Award and two awards at the Brussels Film Festival. *Galaxy Quest*'s scriptwriters, Robert Gordon and David Howard, won a Nebula Award from the Science Fiction and Fantasy Writers of America. And Debra Zane, who was the casting director on the film, was nominated for the Artios Award from the Casting Society of America.

Casting directors are the people responsible for finding the right cast for a movie. A casting director finds out the specific characteristics a movie's producers and director are looking for, and then searches through tons of résumés in order to find the right people to audition for each part.

Galaxy Quest was the movie that really made casting directors take notice of Corbin Bleu. He was only ten years old when the movie was released, and though it wasn't a large role, the movie was really popular.

It was enough to garner the attention of the casting directors at Fox, who were looking for someone to play Austin in a movie they were calling *Mission Without Permission*.

That movie was later called *Catch That Kid*, and it skyrocketed Corbin's fame!

Chapter 5

Corbin's That Kid!

Sometimes described as *"Mission Impossible* for kids," *Catch That Kid*, which premiered in United States movie theaters in 2004, is about a young girl named Maddy, played by Kristen Stewart, whose dad needs to have a crucial operation. Maddy's greatest love is mountain climbing, but her dad won't let her do it anymore.

Maddy recruits her best friends to help her—Gus, who is played by Max Thierot, and Austin, played by Corbin Bleu. The three decide to rob a bank to get the money for Maddy's dad to have the operation he desperately needs after he was injured in a fall while trying to climb Mount Everest.

The reviews of the movie were mixed. Some critics thought it was too similar to the *Spy Kids* trilogy, which was also produced by Fox. But others thought it was a great movie for kids. "*Catch That Kid* is an entertaining family film that has as much appeal for girls as boys because it wisely makes heroes of both sexes," wrote Louis Hobson for the Canadian website Jam Movies. And the movie was well-liked enough to be nominated for a Young Artist Award for Best Feature Family Film (Drama) in 2005.

In *Catch That Kid*, Corbin's character, Austin, is a computer whiz, and Gus is a mechanical genius. Both boys have a crush on Maddy, which makes for lots of conflict between the three friends—it's hard when you like someone your friend also likes! That conflict takes up some time in the movie, but for the most part, *Catch That Kid* is like a James Bond movie for teenagers—it's action-packed. However, when Maddy kisses one of the boys, the other gets jealous. So she conspires to make each boy think she only has eyes for him.

Catch That Kid is a remake of a Danish children's movie from 2002, but its themes are all-American. There's the pretty girl, her two smart guy friends, and a major challenge to overcome. Maddy desperately wants to save her dad, and the dramatic heist seems to be the only way she can do it.

The *New York Times* called *Catch That Kid* "the ultimate 'don't try this at home' movie," and that's pretty obvious—Maddy, Austin, and Gus get into some big-time trouble. The screenplay was written by Derek Haas and Michael Brandt, who also wrote the 2003 action-crime movie *2 Fast 2 Furious*. *Catch That Kid* doesn't have the racy adult themes of *2 Fast 2 Furious*, but it doesn't play it safe, either. Maddy pits her friends against each other in an effort to get them both on her side. And the bank heist, no matter how good the cause may be, certainly isn't the best way to help an ailing father.

Corbin must have had a good time working on the movie with Max Thierot and Kristen Stewart. Kristen, who is a year younger than Corbin, had recently completed work on *Panic Room*, which starred Jodie Foster.

Since filming *Catch That Kid*, Kristen has been in many movies, including *Undertow*, *Fierce People*, and *Zathura*. Teenhollywood.com said that her performance in *Catch That Kid* was like "a young Jennifer Garner." Kristen grew up palling around with her older brother, so she was used to hanging with the guys. It was probably second nature to her to film a movie where she was the only young female character.

Catch This Kid was Max's first major movie. Max is just one year older than Corbin, and since costarring in *Catch That Kid,* has gone on to work on 2005's *The Pacifier,* starring Vin Diesel, and has completed *Jumper* and *Nancy Drew,* which are scheduled to come out in 2007 and 2008. In *Nancy Drew,* Max will star as the young sleuth's romantic interest, Ned Nickerson.

The cast members who starred in *Catch That Kid* were all about the same age, which seems like it would've made for really a fun filming experience! Corbin always enjoys the closeness that working on a movie brings. He counts his costars—past and present—among his close friends.

And the adult actors in *Catch That Kid* are pretty cool, too.

Jennifer Beals portrayed Maddy's mom, Molly. Jennifer is probably most well known for her role in *Flashdance,* the seminal 1980s dance movie, as Alex Owens. But she's also been in other movies, like *The Last Days of Disco, Runaway Jury,* and the horror movie *The Grudge 2.* Currently, she's one of the cast members of the Showtime series *The L Word,* in which she plays Belle Porter.

Interestingly, Jennifer made *Flashdance* when she was in her first year of college at Yale, so she may have had lots of wisdom to offer her young costars on balancing fame with a regular life—something that all young stars seem to struggle with. Jennifer also has an interracial background, with an African-American father and an Irish mother, so that experience may have provided some inspiration for Corbin.

And Sam Robards may have had words of wisdom for Corbin, too. Sam Robards is another actor from *Catch That Kid*. He played Maddy's dad. He's been in lots of movies, including *American Beauty* and *Bright Lights Big City*, and also starred on the TV show *The West Wing*. He's also been on *Sex and the City*, *Spin City*, and *Law and Order*, and was nominated for Broadway's 2002 Tony Award for his role in *The Man Who Had All the Luck*, a play by the famous playwright Arthur Miller.

Like Corbin, Sam's professional acting career began when he was in an off-Broadway play. And also like Corbin, Sam's parents were both actors—his mother, Lauren Bacall, is a fashion icon who was in many movies, including *How to Marry a Millionaire* with Marilyn Monroe. Lauren Bacall was once married to Humphrey Bogart.

And Sam's father was Jason Robards, an Academy Award–winning actor who was in dozens of movies and television shows. Corbin must have had a lot to talk about with Sam.

It isn't just seeing his face on the big screen that appeals to Corbin Bleu. The close relationships he develops with his costars, whether they're his age or much older and more experienced, has been incredibly helpful to him. In his online journal at corbinbleu.com, Corbin wrote in 2006 that he and Kristen and Max were still friends. "And we still keep in contact with each other," he added.

Corbin has said that his favorite medium is definitely movies. He told thestarscoop.com, "With me, everything needs to be fresh. When you do a TV show, it's great, every time you get to dive into your character more and more, but at the same time I kind of feel like, I've already done this. They both have their highs and lows." But after working on a ton of movies in a row, he was ready for a change.

He was headed for television!

Chapter 6

Crash Landing in Paradise!

Before 2005, Corbin had had a few guest spots on television shows, but he'd never had a long-term role. That was before the news went out that a new show called *Flight 29 Down* was looking for teenage actors.

The show, which centers around a group of kids whose small charter plane has crashed somewhere between Guam and the island of Palau, has been often compared to ABC's popular show *Lost*, in which an airplane crashes on its way to Los Angeles from Australia. But fans disagree. The similarities, they say, end at "crashed on an island."

Corbin thinks the show is a mixture of *Lord of the Flies* meets *Gilligan's Island*, according to Family Screen Scene online. "It's survival," he told them. Not only do the kids have to figure out how to get along with one another, but they also have to stay alive in a situation that could easily kill them. We all have seen survival shows on TV, and the situation is usually pretty dire. The characters on *Flight 29 Down* need to survive—and they've also got to find a way to not kill one another.

Corbin plays Nathan on *Flight 29 Down*. Nathan's not exactly like Corbin—he's a Boy Scout, and "he's a little bit of a control freak," Corbin told *Scholastic News Online*. But he's got some really great qualities. Nathan immediately wants to take charge when the kids land in the terrifying, deserted island. In other words, he wants to keep his fellow survivors safe. And though he may not be a natural-born leader, by the end of the first episode, Nathan has decided that the perfect thing for him to do is keep a detailed video recording of their time on the island.

Like Corbin, Nathan is really family-oriented, which is why he wants that leadership role on the island. Corbin told thestarscoop.com, "now that [Nathan's] been stuck on this island, he doesn't have anybody there telling him how good he is as much as he has to prove to himself that he has the chops to be able to lead. When he gets on this island, he wants to become leader. He ends up finding out that a lot of things he does, he constantly messes up, that's not something he's used to. He gets back up on his feet. He's very passionate. I love to lead, and when I fall I get right back up. Nathan is a little bit more dorky."

And Corbin told *Time for Kids*, "I'm like him in a way. I definitely like to lead. I like to take charge of things, and I never really give up on what I do."

As Corbin told *Scholastic News* Online, in Nathan's video diary "he takes his camera and explains to the audience exactly what is going on. [Since] they are stuck on an island, he wants to have a diary in case anything happens."

Nathan's narration of his video diary is also the narration of the show itself, so Corbin has to keep up on everything that's happening on *Flight 29 Down*—not just his own character.

However, Nathan wasn't the character Corbin initially thought he'd play. When he first auditioned for the show, he tried out for the part of Eric. But the *Flight 29 Down* producers thought Corbin would be better as Nathan, and the part of Eric went to Jeremy James Kissner.

When Corbin went in to audition for the Nathan

role, he was able to meet the rest of the cast. Luckily, he gets along really well with his costars. To film *Flight 29 Down*, the cast spends three straight months in a condo on the North Shore of Hawaii's Oahu island, the most popular Hawaiian island. Corbin told KriSeLen.com, "One of the things about us getting along so well is that we can live close to each other without driving each other crazy. The condo gets a little cramped sometimes, but it's cozy and has a great view."

The island is full of great views—it is jam-packed with gorgeous scenery and things to do. It has historical sites, like the site of the Pearl Harbor battlefield from World War II. There's also a ton to do for fun, like snorkeling, swimming, and surfing. Corbin told *Time for Kids*, "It was absolutely amazing! Hawaii is a really beautiful and relaxing place. We had the beach. We had the stars at night. The condo we were staying at was two blocks from the beach. It had a patio roof. We'd go up there every night to watch the sunset and the stars. And we shot the show on the beach."

It's no surprise that Hawaii is a popular place for filmmakers and television executives to use for the making of TV shows and movies. Besides *Flight 29 Down*, the television show *Lost* is also filmed there. So is the popular reality show *Dog the Bounty Hunter*.

In the past, television shows that have utilized the grand landscapes of Hawaii have included *Hawaii 5-0*, *Magnum P.I.*, *North Shore*, and *Raven*. And many shows have used the islands for special episodes, including *Beverly Hills 90210*, *The Brady Bunch*, and *Saved by the Bell*. The movie *50 First Dates* was filmed almost entirely in Hawaii, as were the *Jurassic Park* movies and *Waterworld*.

It makes sense that Hawaii is such a popular place to make movies and TV shows. There are large cities, like Honolulu, in which to film city scenes, and the lush vegetation and animal life on the islands is unparalleled.

Corbin told *Scholastic News*, "You can't even imagine how pretty it is unless you go there. I mean, people can describe it to you, but you can't actually imagine how beautiful it is until you've been there. The sand is like butter and the water is so warm, so great, and so beautiful."

Corbin had never traveled to Hawaii before the shooting of *Flight 29 Down* began. His dad, David, traveled with him for the first month. David and Corbin set up a webcam so that they could communicate between LA and Hawaii over the Internet with ease.

Corbin was lucky to make friends with his costars, especially since they all lived together. He told *Time for Kids*, "The bonding that we got from that was amazing. We saw each other every day at work, and then we'd come home and hang out after work. We had a great time. The cast was really easy to get along with."

When they weren't shooting an episode of *Flight 29 Down*, Corbin and his costars hung out in the condo they shared. They frequently watched movies together, and they had a standing dinner date at a sushi place not far from their condo. And during the rare moments of downtime they had while filming the first season of *Flight 29 Down*, the cast got completely addicted to Boggle. In an interview with starrymag.com, Corbin said, "We would play it between scenes and even during lunch. Now whenever we're together we have to play. Sometimes we have two separate games going on at the same time."

Hallee Hirsh, who was one of Corbin's costars, told teentelevision.com, "It's like a family. We know each other very, very well. We all hang out all the time. I still talk to them every day so that says a lot about how we got along in Hawaii, very well. I consider them some of the closest friends I will ever have."

In a way, the experience of living and working together and spending so much free time together helped the *Flight 29 Down* cast prepare for filming. The seven actors who make up the main cast didn't know one another before being cast on the show. And the teenagers who crash on the Pacific island don't know each other that well, either. But they have to pull together to survive on the island. Of course, they probably don't have Boggle and sushi to look forward to, but over the course of the first season, the characters on *Flight 29 Down* grow as close as the actors playing them did.

The seven young stars of *Flight 29 Down* are Allan Alvarado as Lex, Corbin Bleu as Nathan, Hallee Hirsh as Daley, Jeremy James Kissner as Eric, Johnny Pacar as Jackson, Lauren Storm as Taylor, and Kristy Wu as Melissa.

Allan Alvarado, who plays Lex, is only eleven years old, but he's been on both *Flight 29 Down* and a few episodes of *Cold Case*, as well as the movie *On the Line*.

Hallee Hirsh has had a longer career. She had a fifteen-episode run on *ER*, as well as a seventeen-episode stint on *JAG*. She's also guest-starred on other shows, like *Will and Grace* and *Grey's Anatomy*. While her role on *Flight 29 Down* as Daley is the first time Hallee has been a series regular, her career began in 1994 with a spot on *Saturday Night Live*. Hallee was only seven!

At the age of twenty-one, Jeremy James Kissner (who plays Eric) is one of the older *Flight 29 Down* stars. He's been a guest star on *ER*, and he was also in the monkey movie *Funky Monkey* and the 2001 science-fiction flick *AI*. Jeremy has a movie called *Brotherhood of Blood* in the works.

Johnny Pacar has only been acting since 2002, but in that time he's managed to rack up an impressive list on his acting résumé. He was a guest star for seven episodes of *American Dreams*; he's been on *Tru Calling*, *Medium*, and *Cold Case*. He was also in the movie *Purgatory House*. Even though he plays Jackson, a teenager, Johnny is the oldest of the cast members at the age of twenty-five.

Lauren Storm, who plays Taylor, is the same age as Corbin, and like Corbin, she has an impressive list of credits. She's been on a number of hit TV shows, including *Malcolm in the Middle*, *24*, *CSI: Miami*, and *7th Heaven*. Lauren, who graduated from high school at the young age of sixteen, is also on the board of directors of two charity organizations, Kids With a Cause and Olive Crest. Besides on *Flight 29 Down*, you'll be able to see the popular blond star in the upcoming movie *Together Again for the First Time*, a comedy that also stars Larisa Oleynik and Joseph Lawrence—the big brother of Corbin's costars Andy and Matthew Lawrence from *Family Tree*.

Rounding out the *Flight 29 Down* cast is Kristy Wu as Melissa. Kristy was born in 1982, and her acting career began with a stint on the show *Arli$$* when she was seventeen. Since then, she's been in a few episodes of *Buffy the Vampire Slayer*, as well as small roles on *Freaks and Geeks*, *Joan of Arcadia*, and the Disney movie *Return to Halloweentown*. Lucas Grabeel, Corbin's costar from *High School Musical*, was also in the *Halloweentown* movies. Apparently, Hollywood is a pretty small world!

Flight 29 Down was created by Stan Rogow and D. J. MacHale. Stan Rogow has produced many television shows and movies, including, most famously, *Lizzie McGuire* and *The Lizzie McGuire Movie*, for which he was the executive producer. He's also the executive producer for *Darcy's Wild Life*, a show that many people in the business have referred to as the next *Lizzie McGuire*.

D. J. MacHale, who also directs *Flight 29 Down*, is the writer of the best-selling series of fantasy books *Pendragon*. He has also written, directed, and executive-produced TV shows like *Ghostwriter*, *Are You Afraid of the Dark?*, *Tower of Terror*, and *Chris Cross*, which won a CableAce Award in 1995. In 2006, D. J. was nominated for a Directors Guild of America Award in Outstanding Directorial Achievement in Children's Programs for the episode of *Flight 29 Down* called "The Pits."

Flight 29 Down has proven to be a surprise hit for the executives at Discovery Kids. Rumor has it that the show was pitched first to the Disney Channel, who passed on the idea because the show didn't fit in with their lineup at the time.

But Discovery Kids jumped at the chance to do the show, and they are glad they did: A survey of American kids ages eight to fifteen, held after the kids watched the first two episodes of the series, was the "best in Discovery Kids' history," one of the show's producers told the *Honolulu Star-Bulletin*.

In fact, the show was green-lit for a second season before the first season even aired in the United States. So Corbin was right when he told *Time for Kids*, "Kids are going to love the show because it shows them that whatever situation they're put into, they can get through it. It's all about working together as a team to try to survive. I think kids will relate to the teens on the show. It has a compilation of pretty much everything. There's drama, but there's also lots of comic relief in it." *Flight 29 Down* is so popular, in fact, that a series of books has been created to tie in to the television show.

Flight 29 Down's world premiere took place at Sunset on the Beach, a huge outdoor theater in Hawaii. Unfortunately, just before the showing took place, a huge rainstorm hit. But that didn't stop the locals from staying to watch the first two half-hour episodes. Ann Larson, a Honolulu resident, told the *Honolulu Advertiser*, "It came out really, really well. I'm really proud that this came from Hawaii."

There's no word yet on whether we'll get a third season of *Flight 29 Down*, but even the people of Hawaii hope the cast will be back on the island to film more shows soon. And the cast does, too! In an interview with the *Honolulu Advertiser*, Corbin's costar Lauren Storm said, "It's totally rare that you find an ensemble cast that really cares about each other. And it's great to be doing this in Hawaii."

Corbin agreed, telling StarryConstellation.com, "The island's beauty and serenity is something that can't be imagined unless you experience it for yourself."

Corbin and his cast mates probably wish they could live in Hawaii all year round, relaxing, hanging out, and, of course, surfing. Corbin loves to surf and was successful at it the very first time he tried—no small feat, especially in Hawaii, where the waves can crest incredibly high. He credits his history in dance for that talent. He told the *Honolulu Advertiser*, "I'm very coordinated because I've been dancing my whole life. I loved surfing. You're literally standing on water—totally Cloud Nine."

Believe it or not, though, it only takes three months to film a season of *Flight 29 Down*. Young actors generally fill the hiatus—the break from filming—with industry events, catching up on school, and, whenever possible, picking up new work. Corbin seems to be one of those up-and-comers who can never sit still, and so during the break between the first two seasons of *Flight 29 Down*, he headed back to California . . . and straight into a casting call with Disney, who was putting together the cast for a little movie called *High School Musical*.

Chapter 7
Back to School!

Musicals have been popular for centuries. But the last really great teen musical was *Grease*, from the 1970s. *Grease* is the quintessential American story of a good girl who falls in love with a bad boy. And even *Grease*, with its drinking and flirting, wasn't exactly innocent. The executives at the Disney Channel realized there was a need for a new musical—something that could be entertaining and innocent at the same time. It's been a while since a musical was as globally popular as *High School Musical* became. Musicals were seen as clichéd; most teenagers never really got excited about them.

The new musical Disney had in mind needed to appeal to Disney's core group of fans—young teenagers who would be galvanized by the music and the story line. The musical needed to be wholesome, to fit in with the network's other shows. Parents needed to approve of the movie, but Disney wanted it to also be something teens of today would identify with. And the most important thing, Disney knew, was to put together the right group of people—both in front of and behind the camera. The casting was incredibly important, but the right people had to be behind the scenes, too, in order to make *High School Musical* a huge hit.

Disney turned to Bill Borden, who had produced *In the Mix*, among other movies, and Barry Rosenbush, the producer of *Scary Movie 2*. Bill Borden understood Disney's idea for the movie from the start. He told the *Florida Sun-Sentinel*, "I wanted to make a film that didn't speak down to anyone."

Along with Don Schain, who had produced other Disney movies, and director Kenny Ortega, the accomplished choreographer behind such seminal dance scenes as the parade scene in *Ferris Bueller's Day Off* and much of the movie *Dirty Dancing*, as well as *Pretty in Pink* and the opening ceremony for the 2000 Olympics, the team set out to create the perfect teenage musical movie.

Kenny was a large part of the reason the movie

would eventually become incredibly popular, according to Ashley Tisdale. She told MediaVillage.com, "Kenny had an amazing vision and made it all come to life. He was very respectful toward the kids, listening to us and having us tell him what we thought would be good. He was very open to our opinions and stuff. I think that's maybe why it did so well."

The creators of *High School Musical* drew from many sources of inspiration to put the movie together. Bill Borden told the *Florida Sun-Sentinel*, "I drew from a lot of things. I love Franco Zeffirelli's *Romeo and Juliet*. That was one of my biggest influences, seeing that when I was a freshman in high school. The whole balcony scene in [*High School Musical*] was influenced by that."

You can't go wrong with one of the most classic love stories of all time, right? But the creators of *High School Musical* didn't want the movie to feel stuffy or old, either. They also took some inspiration from *Grease*. Gary Marsh, the Disney Channel president of entertainment, told the *San Francisco Chronicle*, "It's *Romeo and Juliet* meets *Grease*. But we said, let's set it in contemporary times."

And it turned out that contemporary flavor was

just what Disney needed to achieve its largest, most successful TV movie of all time. The script for *High School Musical* doesn't have a very complicated story line—it's pretty much a boy-meets-girl story, with a little basketball and science thrown in. It turns out that a movie doesn't have to have an overly complicated story line to appeal to viewers.

The romantic comedy's script was written by Peter Barsocchini. He set the movie at the fictitious East High in Albuquerque, New Mexico. Peter wanted to write a movie that would appeal to people of all ages, and according to Corbin, he did. Corbin told California's NBC-11, "It's really a family-oriented movie. I've actually had people in their fifties and sixties come up to me and say, 'We loved your movie,' and I'm like, 'Wow!' It's so great that everybody is able to relate to it."

It's fairly rare that adults and teenagers can gather together to enjoy a movie. That, of course, is part of the power of *High School Musical*. Of course, part of it is also the incredible musical numbers.

A number of different songwriters worked on the songs in *High School Musical*, which in turn created a number of different-feeling songs. The songs don't all blend together; they each have their own flavor.

Ken Tucker, a critic at *Entertainment Weekly*, told CBSnews.com that there was a surprise element to *High School Musical* that helped its success. "I think that when you're a young person in school these days you're part of a clique, and it's a very potent thing to see a TV movie that shows cliques can be broken through, go from being a nerd to being part of the popular crowd. It's one of those 'crossing the boundaries' things that's very appealing to young audiences."

The film's overarching message is that it is okay to be different. It's okay that love interests superjock Troy Bolton and brainiac Gabriella Montez have separate interests—they can like each other, anyway. It's okay to be yourself, no matter who that might be. Feeling at peace with yourself is something that a lot of teens struggle with. It can be really hard to feel like you're different from other people. The message from *High School Musical*, which lots of teenagers feel really grateful for, is that not only is it okay to be yourself—it's great!

Kenny Ortega, *High School Musical*'s director, told the *San Francisco Chronicle* that he was drawn to the movie's premise because he related to it. "I was an athlete who was torn between track and dance," he said. "I was a kid who was bullied. I saw this character Troy looking for the courage to step forward and be fearless and say, 'I'm this, too,' and that really hit home."

That innocent fearlessness is a far cry from many other teen movies. Bill Bolton told *Newsweek* that *High School Musical*, too, isn't afraid to be different. He didn't want to make yet another movie about someone changing themselves to become popular. "I wanted to make a movie that we could watch over and over as a family. The nature of the characters is right out of mythological storytelling. It is classical *Romeo and Juliet*, searching for one's identity . . . cliques in society and how you have to behave."

In other words, the movie speaks straight to that normal teenage feeling of insecurity. And parents can relate to that—after all, they were teenagers once, and went through many of the same things. And thanks to the family-friendly style of Disney programming, parents can watch *High School Musical* with their kids, without feeling like the movie is too young and boring or too adult and inappropriate for younger kids. From the second the script was completed, Disney knew that *High*

School Musical was just right for their particular brand of television.

They did not know, however, the magnitude of the hit they were about to have on their hands. *High School Musical* only cost $4.5 million dollars to make— that's a pretty small budget for a full-length feature film, especially one with such a large cast. And most of the people behind the scenes didn't think the movie would be hugely successful. They knew it would do well and appeal to their demographic. But they had no idea it would be one of their most successful ventures of all time, and cause a cultural tidal wave of fame for the movie's stars.

And speaking of the movie's stars, they still hadn't been cast! So with the producers, music, and script ready, the casting call went out . . .

Chapter 8

Casting Call

With *High School Musical*, Disney had unknowingly created the perfect equation for a hit movie. They had a great, feel-good story line that parents wouldn't worry about having their kids watch, a story that had a great message for people of all ages. They had proven talent in their executive producers and director. And they had music that made everyone want to sing along.

Now they needed a cast. A casting call was sent out, to which anyone who was interested could respond and then show up at auditions. But Corbin was obviously ahead of most kids his age, since he had been working for over a decade before *High School Musical* was even a glimmer in Disney's eye. The competition was stiff, though. Hundreds of actors wanted to be part of the next Disney Channel original movie.

Corbin had what it took to be cast in the movie. His background in musical theater really helped. At his high school, he had played the lead in *Footloose*, and he'd also been in *Grease*. That showed that he understood the genre. His great singing voice helped prove that he had the vocal chops to participate in all of the musical numbers. He had been in movies before, so he was no stranger to the kind of work it would take to put together a full-length feature film. And he had the good looks to keep viewers interested.

Corbin's dance skills, too, impressed the casting agents. He'd studied dance for years, including with the famous dancer Debbie Allen. As Corbin told *Time for Kids*, "Dancing is something I've been doing since I was two years old. I've taken classes everywhere. It was really cool to be able to use my abilities in a movie. It's the first musical movie that I've ever done. I have a background in musical theater, so it was really cool to be able to incorporate that into a movie."

Corbin was lucky to be cast with a great group of costars. Zac Efron and Vanessa Hudgens were cast as Troy Bolton and Gabriella Montez, who are love interests from totally different social groups at East High. Ashley

Tisdale, who is best known for her work as sweet Maddie on Disney's *The Suite Life of Zack & Cody*, was cast as mean girl Sharpay. Lucas Grabeel played Sharpay's brother, Ryan. And Monique Coleman was cast as Taylor McKessie.

Though Corbin originally tried out for the role of Ryan, he was cast as Chad Danforth, Troy's best friend. Corbin told *Scholastic News* online, "I originally auditioned for Lucas's role, but I couldn't shake my hips as well as Lucas could. They felt I was better for the role of Chad."

Many of the new cast members had Disney ties. Ashley Tisdale stars on *The Suite Life of Zack & Cody*, and Vanessa Hudgens and Monique Coleman have been on the show as well. Lucas Grabeel had been in *Halloweentown High* and *Return to Halloweentown*, both Disney movies.

The cast got along great from the beginning. Ashley Tisdale told tommy2.net, "It was so much fun. . . . We just kind of bonded and I have all these new friends and we're really excited to see everybody's reaction, because for us it's really cool."

Even outsiders saw that the casting had been well done from the beginning. Variety.com said, "Kudos should be given to the casting agents who so evenly rounded out the cast with appealing characters, particularly Corbin Bleu as Troy's friend and teammate Chad, and Monique Coleman as academic overachiever Taylor."

Corbin's role as Chad Danforth was very different from the role he had been playing on *Flight 29 Down*. Corbin told KriSeLen.com, "The character I played [in *High School Musical*] was also a fun change. I usually end up playing some form of nerd, so to play a jock was great. The whole experience was amazing."

For one thing, Chad was a jock. He had basketball moves that Corbin definitely did not. But true to form, Corbin learned the rules of the game as quickly as possible. Corbin told *Scholastic News* online, "Chad is very into basketball. I'm similar to Chad in the way that he has a strong passion for what he does. But I'm kind of sports-challenged. Give me a ball and I don't know what to do with the thing! But I worked really hard and by the end I was very comfortable with the ball."

He wasn't the only one who had things to learn on the set. Ashley Tisdale could barely dance before she walked in to the first day of rehearsal. She told *Scholastic News* online, "I'm really uncoordinated with dance, but [director Kenny Ortega] made us all into dancers."

Once casting was set, everyone buckled down to make the movie. They flew to Salt Lake City to film, though the movie is set in Albuquerque, New Mexico. They started off with two weeks of incredibly intense training. Luckily, the group bonded quickly, making the beginning work seem . . . well, less like work, and more like hanging out with good friends. They'd move from exercise to basketball to dance classes, working on all the moves that would make the great, high-energy choreography in *High School Musical*.

Zac Efron told *Scholastic News* online, "We had two weeks of intense dancing, acting, singing, and basketball rehearsals along with strange stretching [exercises] and things I'd never heard of before. We'd wake up at six in the morning and work until six at night. It was a very long day, but by the end I'd sustained so many injuries and was so sore but so much better than I was before. I learned more in those two weeks than I'd learned in the previous years. Every second of it was worth it."

After the training portion was over, they began working on the film itself. They had four weeks of what's known as "principal photography," which translates to the actual filming of the movie. It's kind of amazing that it took four weeks to create a movie that's over in less than two hours, but it did! After each day was over, the cast would hang out. Zac Efron told *Time for Kids*, "It was a blast. The whole cast would hang out after every day of shooting. We'd go out and eat dinner and we just did fun stuff together and it made being on the set a lot more fun."

In fact, the energy from working and dancing together during the day carried over into the night. The cast would go to movies and out to dinner, or just hang out in one another's hotel rooms, talking and having a good time. But there were occasional bursts of crazy fun that can happen only on a Hollywood set. Corbin told StarryMag.com, "After having a great day filming and hanging out at dinner, the cast came into the hotel pretty late. We were all still very excited from the day, so to get out the rest of our energy, we performed the dance finale in the middle of the hotel lobby." Wouldn't it have been cool to be in the hotel that day?

The energy of the cast shows up in the film, too. Lots of kids love the movie because it seems so real—everyone in the movie looks like they're having fun, and the truth is, they probably are! Every person who worked on the movie knew it was something to be proud of. But they had no idea just how popular *High School Musical* would be . . . and what adventures were in store for the coming year.

Chapter 9

High School Musical: The Legend

Nearly eight million people tuned in to watch the premiere of *High School Musical* on January 20, 2006. Disney had been actively promoting the show for weeks, but they had no idea they'd get so many viewers. The over seven million people who watched *High School Musical* that night helped set a Disney record. It also made the show the top-rated cable broadcast (excluding sports programs) for January 2006. As if that wasn't enough, *High School Musical* earned the highest ratings of all cable movies that month. And that was just the beginning.

Disney had not expected that kind of success, and truth be told, neither did the stars of *High School Musical*. Vanessa Hudgens told CBSNews.com, "We had no idea that it was going to be this big but we got lucky; it turned out to be a phenomenon. Musicals haven't been done in such a long time for kids; it's something new."

But Zac Efron had the feeling that *High School Musical* would be a huge hit. He told MediaVillage.com, "Going into the production, you could tell there was a lot of momentum behind the movie. Everyone was very enthusiastic while we made the film, which is uncharacteristic of a lot of movies. The cast and crew were very excited the whole time we were making it and that came through on camera. I hoped it would do as well as it's done. I'm ecstatic."

He wasn't the only one thrilled by the success. Fans were happy, too, because the initial success of the movie meant more *High School Musical* products, promotions, and, of course, showings on the Disney Channel. Within the first month it was shown on the Disney Channel, more than twenty-six million people tuned in to see *High School Musical*. Some of them were fans who couldn't get enough; some were parents, wanting to know what the fuss was about.

Surprisingly, when the reviews came in, they were mixed. *Variety* wrote, "High school is a time when kids are just beginning to discover their true selves in an environment where individuality is as welcome as leprosy. To express this notion with fresh dialogue is one thing, but to convey it through song is a marvel."

Kevin Carr from the website 7mpictures.com agreed. He wrote, "*High School Musical* is a fun piece, and the music is surprisingly catchy. . . . I can see where the mixture of music and teen drama has touched so many kids. Probably the biggest strength of *High School Musical* is its wholesomeness, for lack of a better term. Sure, it's made by Disney, but I never got the sense they were trying to make a wholesome film. Rather, the filmmakers were just trying to tell a story. Sex, drugs, and violence just didn't factor into that equation. *High School Musical* is a fine film for families to watch, and you won't get embarrassed."

And *Entertainment Weekly*, which gave *High School Musical* a B+, said, "*High School Musical*, with its big throbbing heart, gives out all the right messages without being slow-witted or preachy."

But in stark contrast, the *New York Times* wrote, "There are those who may make the argument that young viewers are such idiots that they need constant repetition and wild exaggeration to get whatever point a story is trying to make. And it would be unfair not to salute the movie's message about broadening one's horizons and not being limited by stereotypes or peer pressure. But when an admirable message is packaged in such treacle, it just makes the message seem treacly, too."

It just goes to show you that reviewers simply cannot predict with any certainty whether a movie will do well or not. The very things that the *New York Times* panned were the things that made *High School Musical* so appealing to viewers. No matter what the reviews said, teens and tweens—and their parents—couldn't get enough of *High School Musical*. Whatever the reason people were watching, they just kept on watching. Since it premiered in January 2006, *High School Musical* has been rebroadcast well over a dozen times on the Disney Channel.

But the TV version was just the first piece of the huge *High School Musical* pie. The sound track to the movie was also a huge hit.

A few weeks before the movie premiered on the Disney Channel, the network began spotlighting the music from *High School Musical*. They also released some of the sound track's songs online, and even ran a promotion for free downloads of the song "Breaking Free," performed by Zac Efron and Vanessa Hudgens, with a code that could be found at bus stations and in malls. A week before the movie was first on television, the sound track was released on CD.

The Disney Channel also began showing music videos of the sound track's singles, and Radio Disney picked up the songs, broadcast on its more than fifty AM and FM stations nationwide. That was enough to start the buzz—not just for the premiere of *High School Musical*, but also to showcase the movie's multitalented stars, who perform all of the songs on the album.

The album debuted at number 143 on the *Billboard* charts, which ranks copies of CDs sold. It sold only about six thousand copies in its first week. But just three weeks after its release, the *High School Musical* sound track was number 10, and it hit the number 1 spot twice, both times in March 2006. By August, more than three million copies of the sound track had been sold. The album had officially gone triple platinum.

In fact, it was the best-selling album released in 2006. Gil Kaufman, a writer for Vh1.com, wrote, "New albums by big stars top the *Billboard* chart just about every week. What doesn't happen that often—okay, never before—is for the sound track of a kids' TV movie to debut near the bottom of the top 200 on sales of 6,500 copies, only to climb to number 58 the next week, then crack the top 10 and hit number 1 after seven weeks. It just doesn't happen."

The success of the sound track to a made-for-TV movie had highbrow music critics all over America wondering what was going on. It was the first time a TV sound track had cracked the big list since the *Miami Vice* sound track in the mid-1980s. Even the bigwigs at Disney hadn't seen that extra success coming. Damon Whiteside, who is the vice president of marketing for Walt Disney Records, told MTV.com, "What's most amazing is that six weeks into its release, it's number 1. Most albums debut big and decrease. We knew it was going to be a success, but we didn't think it would be this big a phenomenon."

In total, nine of the songs on the *High School Musical* sound track have made it to the *Billboard* Top 100. Ashley Tisdale is one of the few female artists to ever have two songs at the same time debuting in the Top 100. She told tommy2.net, "It was really cool, it was a dream come true because I really wanted to record and

73

do an album one day."

To further the hype behind the music from *High School Musical*, the day after the movie premiered on the Disney Channel, the network aired a special sing-along version of the movie. Viewers tuned in to see the movie again, obviously, but they were in for a treat—the lyrics to the songs were shown at the bottom of the television screen so that newly minted fans could sing along at home.

A month later, Disney staged a dance-along version as well. The stars of the now-hit movie appeared to teach viewers all the moves to two of the most popular songs, "Get'cha Head in the Game" and "We're All in This Together."

Five months after the American and Canadian premiere on January 20, 2006, *High School Musical* went international. The Australian version kicked things off, premiering on Australia's Disney Channel on June 10, 2006. The Asian affiliate was next, and then the movie was shown in Brazil, Germany, Norway, Sweden, Denmark, the Middle East, France, England, India, Portugal, Italy, Spain, Taiwan, Chile, the Netherlands, South Africa, and Venezuela. All told, by the end of November 2006, *High*

School Musical had been seen on six continents!

The cast was overwhelmed and grateful to their fans—and, of course, to Disney. Ashley Tisdale told *Scholastic News* online why she thought the movie was such a huge hit. "I think the connection, the chemistry, the support from Disney—it's *Grease* for our generation. It's the music and all of it put together."

But even worldwide fame wasn't the end of the awards and accolades for *High School Musical*. The DVD was released in May 2006, and soon after, the Emmy nominations were announced.

In July 2006, *High School Musical* was nominated for an astounding six Emmy Awards: Outstanding Casting for a Miniseries, Movie, or Special; Outstanding Choreography; Outstanding Directing for a Miniseries, Movie, or Special; Outstanding Music and Lyrics (two nominations, for "Get'cha Head in the Game" and "Breaking Free"); and Outstanding Children's Program.

High School Musical would go on to win the Emmy for Outstanding Children's Program and for Outstanding Choreography. But the Emmys weren't the only awards in store for the musical. It also picked up the Television Critics Association's Award for Excellence in

Children's Programming. And in August 2006, the votes of teenagers across America gave *High School Musical* the Teen's Choice Awards for Choice Comedy/Musical, Best TV Chemistry (for Zac Efron and Vanessa Hudgens), and Choice Breakthrough Star (for Zac Efron).

The cast couldn't believe they'd won Emmy Awards. Corbin wrote in his journal at corbinbleu.com, "All of us are so grateful for all of the success that *High School Musical* has achieved and are also kind of in shock to have won an Emmy at this age. That was my first time at the Emmys and to say that we actually won is mind-boggling to me."

Going to red-carpet awards shows was a new experience for Corbin. He was starstruck at the Teen Choice Awards, too, writing, "At the Teen Choice Awards I had to go backstage to do press just before my idol Johnny Depp came out onstage to receive his award. So I'm kind of bummed that I missed him, but the fact that I was accepting an award at the same venue he was is very rewarding to me."

And the fame just kept building. *Teen People* named the cast in its annual Hottest 25 Under 25 issue, and a special karaoke version of the *High School Musical*

DVD was released. The cast was asked to participate in the Macy's Thanksgiving Day Parade in New York City. They also went to Europe and Australia to promote the film. The screenplay is being re-envisioned as a stage show for high schools to perform.

And to bring *High School Musical* to fans all over America, the cast went on a huge, live concert tour, starting in November 2006, with plans to continue till January 2007. Minus Zac Efron, who was busy filming the remake of the movie *Hairspray* in Canada, the entire cast traveled to more than thirty cities all over the country, performing hit songs from the show as well as songs from their own solo albums. (Zac was replaced for the tour by the actor Drew Seeley.)

Corbin loved having the opportunity to perform the hits from *High School Musical* onstage in front of an audience. He wrote in his journal at corbinbleu.com, "The extra surprise about the tour is that Vanessa, Ashley, and myself now all have recording contracts, and we will be performing some songs from our albums. I am so excited to have the opportunity to perform songs off my new album."

So, what's next for the *High School Musical* legacy?

A sequel, which fans have been clamoring for since the original aired, is planned, though Disney executives are keeping their lips sealed about the release date (they think it will be in late 2007 or 2008). In the sequel, the original cast reprises their roles as the *High School Musical* teens on summer break.

"To be able to experience it all over again will be awesome," Corbin told teenpeople.com.

We couldn't agree more.

Chapter 10

Corbin Jumps In!

After the huge success of *High School Musical*, Disney knew they had a good thing with Corbin Bleu. And Corbin felt the same way. "Disney is really great," he told thestarscoop.com. "Once you do one Disney thing, you're in their pack. You get to do a lot."

In some ways, the Disney Channel is a lot like a big family. Corbin was able to guest star on the premiere episode of the hit TV show *Hannah Montana* with Miley Cyrus in 2006.

He's also been in heavy rotation on the channel, with a special preview of his first music video, "Push It to the Limit," airing over Thanksgiving weekend in 2006.

Corbin also was able to participate in the first annual Disney Channel Games during the summer of 2006, during which his Blue Team took the championship with an astounding 900 points to the Green Team's 725 and the Red Team's 700. Since his *High School Musical* costars Lucas Grabeel and Ashley Tisdale were on the Green Team, and Corbin, Vanessa Hudgens, and Monique Coleman were on the Blue Team, we're sure there was plenty of friendly rivalry between the teams.

And besides all that, during the summer of 2006, Corbin was also signed up for a new movie, *Jump In!*, which premiered on the Disney Channel in January 2007.

Jump In! marked Corbin's first solo starring role in a movie. Izzy Daniels, Corbin's character, is a young boxer. His dad was a boxer, too, and Izzy is following in his dad's footsteps. At the beginning of the movie, Izzy is in training for the prestigious Golden Glove Award, which his dad had also won.

But when his friend Mary convinces him to join a double-Dutch tournament with her, Izzy realizes that he might actually be more partial to jumping rope than to boxing.

Mary is played by Keke Palmer, who is just fourteen years old. She had her acting debut in *Barbershop 2*, and her first starring role as Akeelah Anderson in 2006's *Akeelah and the Bee*.

The movie also stars *Hannah Montana*'s Shanica

CORBIN BLEU

Corbin lookin' smooth on the red carpet

Corbin with his *High School Musical* costar Vanessa Hudgens

Say cheese, Corbin!

Corbin goofing off with Monique Coleman backstage at the Billboard Music Awards

The cast of *High School Musical*

What a smile!

Knowles as well as Elle Downs, Sarah Francis, Paula Brancati, Alessandra Cannito, and Mazin Elsadig. And, of course, in the role of Izzy's father, Kenneth Daniels, is Corbin's real-life dad, David Reivers.

It was a dream come true for Corbin when his dad was cast in *Jump In!* Even though Corbin and David have both been acting for years, it was the first time they worked together. Corbin wrote in his online journal at corbinbleu.com, "Working with my dad was definitely one of the highlights of my career thus far. Being real father and son gave the performance such a true natural life, and gave me such a thrill that I'm sad it's over. Hopefully in the future we will have the opportunity to work together again."

As in many of his roles, Corbin's role as Izzy required him to learn some new skills. For *High School Musical*, he learned the basics of basketball. And in *Jump In!*, he needed to learn how to jump rope like a pro.

Jumping rope might make people think of little girls on the playground, but the sport has gained popularity in recent years. It's also a big part of hip-hop culture. Double Dutch requires four players: Two turn the ropes, and two jump at the same time, often while reciting rhymes along with the beat of the ropes. It's a great way to exercise. There's even a national organization, the National Double Dutch League, which sponsors double Dutch camps and an annual Holiday Classic. At the Holiday Classic, teams from all corners of the globe gather to compete. And some rope-skipping organizations are lobbying to be included in the Olympics.

While filming *Jump In!* in Toronto, Canada, Corbin watched competitive jump-roping competitions at the bi-annual Maple Leaf International and Worlds held in Toronto by the International Rope Skipping Federation. Some footage for *Jump In!* was shot there, since the Worlds is the competition Izzy's team aspires to be in. Corbin also met some teenage girls who were competing there. The team, from North Carolina, told the *Cary News* that meeting Corbin was one of the highlights of their trip. In fact, two of the girls on the Cary team were cast in small roles in *Jump In!*

To train for the movie, Corbin had to work out a lot. In fact, he got into the best shape of his life training at the Wild Card Gym in Los Angeles. He trained with Bridgett "Baby Doll" Riley, a boxer who has worked on other movies, including *Million Dollar Baby*.

Corbin admitted that it wasn't easy to get into such good shape. He wrote in his online journal, "Boxing alone includes single jump roping, strength workout circuits, speed and heavy bags, weight lifting, and of course, working in the ring. On top of that, double Dutch isn't just stepping back and forth. I've been working on difficult tricks inside the ropes such as flips, push-ups, and even splits. It really is incredible. I give boxers and jumpers so much credit for all the hard work they endure."

The film also features real-life double Dutch teams, like the Japanese team Ashigarami. Teen double-Dutchers from all over America were asked to join in the making of the movie.

Being new to a skill has never stopped Corbin Bleu. Not only was he learning the tricks of the double Dutch trade, Corbin had to learn to box in order to film *Jump In!* with convincing skills. Boxing is well known as a sport of strength and power, but not many people know that it is a form of martial arts (like karate or judo). Some people think that boxing first developed in 4000 B.C.E. in North Africa, and there is definite evidence that it was in the Mediterranean area by 1500 B.C.E.

It was really different back then, though. For one

thing, the competitors were usually naked; for another, unlike modern-day boxing, the match would only end when one of the fighters was killed.

Now, there are strict rules in place to protect both fighters from major injury and, of course, from death. Both competitors wear gloves to soften the blow of their fists, and there are regulations in place for areas of the body that are legal to strike. Illegal strikes can result in disqualification. Some well-known boxers are Muhammed Ali, George Foreman, and Sugar Ray Robinson.

Boxing is so potentially dangerous that it's been banned in a number of countries, including Norway, Iceland, and Iran. Obviously, while working on *Jump In!*, Corbin was surrounded by people who were there to keep him safe. And he did hours and hours of training to make sure he was doing everything properly. In true Corbin style, even though he had no boxing or double Dutch experience before filming, that didn't stop him from lighting up the screen with his newfound skills.

One thing Corbin does know how to do, though, is dance. He was spotlighted in the national *High School Musical* traveling tour, both dancing while doing double Dutch onstage, and then shadowboxing. His performance of his new single, "Push It," was one of the highlights of the show for many fans. Corbin's fans are already clamoring for his album, set to hit the stores in April 2007.

Chapter 11
Another Side of Corbin Bleu

As soon as he'd put down his boxing gloves and hung up his jump rope, Corbin was in a recording studio, working on his new album, which is called *Another Side*.

It was high time to show the fans another side of Corbin Bleu. Sure, he was a talented actor. Sure, he was able to pick up new sports skills with great ease. And we knew he had a background in musical theater. But nobody knew he was destined for pop fame, too!

Corbin announced the news to his fans on his online journal at corbinbleu.com as soon as the ink was dry on his record deal. He wrote, "It's so weird because the music industry is new territory for me. I've been singing for a long time, but never professionally. So I'm just giving it my all, hoping for the best, and singing my heart out."

Corbin was among major supporters even when he started out in the new world of the music industry. He was signed by Hollywood Records, one of the record labels owned by Buena Vista Music Group, which in turn is part of the Walt Disney Company.

Hollywood Records has also produced albums by Hilary Duff, The Cheetah Girls, Jesse McCartney, and Raven-Symoné. It's pretty much the go-to label for young teenage stars looking to make it big in music—and it seems to work. Hilary Duff's albums have nearly all gone platinum, and her 2005 album *Most Wanted* debuted in the United States at number one. In a way, she'll be competition for Corbin's record. They'll both release in April 2007. But with Disney behind them, both stars are sure to please listeners and do really well.

Corbin has a wide variety of musical influences. He credits his mom with exposing him to a lot of eighties music, which is his favorite. He told KriSeLen.com, "If it can get me up and grooving, I like it." It's easy to imagine that he likes the high energy and poppy beats of eighties music, since his attitude is so fresh and optimistic.

But at times, everyone needs to chill out—even busy, driven types like Corbin. For those times, he told

Time for Kids, "I'm really into lyrical, soulful, R&B-type music." Sounds like his musical tastes are pretty well-rounded, and his album is said to be a blend of R&B and pop music, with good vibes and a positive message.

He also has a lot of respect for Prince, the influential musician famous for songs like "Little Red Corvette," "Let's Go Crazy," and "Purple Rain." Prince was also an actor, starring in the movies *Graffiti Bridge* and *Purple Rain*. He's also directed movies, composed songs for movie sound tracks, and has produced albums and songs by some of the most famous names in the music business, including Patti LaBelle and Chaka Khan.

While Prince has had a long, controversial career, he has been critically acclaimed. Corbin was able to see Prince on his "Musicology" tour in 2004; the younger performer counts it among the most amazing experiences of his life.

Another of Corbin's influences is Kanye West, the Grammy Award–winning rapper who has had many number-one hits, including 2005's "Gold Digger." Kanye is a born-again Christian, and Corbin, too, identifies as Christian. He may feel more drawn to Kanye because of the faith that they both share.

Combined, these three kinds of influences can all be seen having their effects on Corbin's music. He might have gotten some of his pop beats from eighties music. Listening to Prince may have made him braver and more driven in terms of musical originality. And Kanye West's bravery and soul have definitely shown themselves in Corbin's music. And of course, Corbin's background in musical theater has helped him add an element of playfulness and style to everything he does.

When *Teen Magazine* asked Corbin who his dream tour mate was, he replied that he'd love to go on tour with Beyoncé. But he didn't say whether that was for her talent or her good looks! He just said, "I would love that."

Corbin's first music video, for "Push It to the Limit," premiered on the Disney Channel on November 22, 2006. "Push It to the Limit" also debuted on Radio Disney on the same day. The song, from the sound track to *Jump In!*, is already a hit. And the video was already circulating on the Internet the very day it played on television.

The singles from *High School Musical* that he sang in, "We're All in This Together" and "Stick to the Status Quo," have been listed in *Billboard*'s Top 100, so Corbin's no stranger to knowing he's been a part of hit music.

But as he told TheShowBuzz.com, "Even though I sang in *High School Musical*, I didn't have any solos, so nobody's really heard me sing. So this is *Another Side* of me people will get to see."

However, in his first solo venture, there's more to lose. Corbin stays positive, though. He feels like he's got something fans—and potential fans—want. It's partly just his natural charm, and partly his talent . . . but it's definitely taken him tons of work to get where he is.

And beginning a musical career wasn't easy for him, either. Despite the support he got from Disney, and the confidence that came from his years of formal musical training, recording an album was difficult.

Corbin felt like he had a lot to learn. It took him a while to get comfortable. When he was in the middle of recording *Another Side*, he told *Teen Magazine* online, "It was hard for me at first. . . . It's a whole new learning process for me, but I've been getting more comfortable and confident."

Luckily, he had Matthew Gerard, one of the producers he'd worked with on *High School Musical*, around to make him feel more comfortable. Corbin was used to working with Matthew, so having him in the recording studio was helpful. "[Matthew is] a really cool guy," he told *Teen Magazine* online.

Since he's such a professional, Corbin was able to have a hand in the making of his album. Lots of young stars are told what to sing and how to sing it, but not this guy—in fact, Corbin was involved in the creative process of songwriting as well as singing. He cowrote five of the songs on *Another Side*.

That kind of creative freedom is really important for a young star, but it seems as though it's especially important for a guy like Corbin. He's been working since he was two, which is longer than a lot of adults have had their jobs. If there's one thing Corbin knows how to do, it's perform. Being able to perform on his own terms is very important.

Corbin has never lacked for independence, after all. He tackled the music industry the way he's tackled everything else: with professionalism, charm, and style.

Chapter 12

Corbin Gives Back

Celebrity comes with a price. Those who have climbed to the peaks of fame generally have to give up much of their privacy and their right to any sort of secrecy, and learn to live in the public eye.

However, celebrities are often in a position to give back to the community that has given them so much. Some offer money; some do free commercials; some stage benefits in which the proceeds go to needy people or other causes.

Some celebrities feel that since they have been so lucky, to have a career doing something that they are passionate about, it is their duty to return some of that passion to the community that has supported them.

Corbin is one of those celebrities. Corbin told Disney's Adventures All-Stars, a Disney site devoted to volunteering, "Pretty much any time I can do community service, I do it."

In 2005, Corbin was one of a number of volunteers serving a special Christmas dinner to the homeless just before Christmas Day. With stars like Billy Bush, Jeremy Renner, Ashley Edner, Lauren Storm, Jennifer Love Hewitt, and Texas Battle, Corbin—whose first professional role was as a homeless boy in the off-Broadway play *Tiny Tim Is Dead*—served up a scrumptious dinner at the Los Angeles Mission's annual Christmas meal on December 23, 2005.

Along with other volunteers, Corbin dished up plates of traditional holiday foods to the homeless of Los Angeles's Skid Row district. Four hundred volunteers show up each year to help the Mission serve the homeless. They also handed out Christmas presents to the kids who came to participate in the meal.

The Mission, which was founded in 1936 by Reverend I. L. Eldridge, is one of the nation's largest places of support for the homeless. It is a nonprofit, faith-based organization.

Christianity is an important part of Corbin's life, and since Christmas is also his favorite holiday, the volunteer opportunity was perfect for him. It was not just a way to celebrate Christmas; it was a way to share the holiday with those less fortunate than he is.

Corbin takes part in a number of holiday-related volunteer opportunities. In 2006, he attended the annual Christmas tree-lighting extravaganza at Los Angeles's The Grove, which is one of his favorite places to hang out. The tree-lighting kicks off the Season of Wishes campaign, headed by the Make-A-Wish Foundation.

The Make-A-Wish Foundation grants wishes to kids with terminal diseases—the children often wish to meet a celebrity, for example, and the foundation makes that wish come true. Other celebrities at the November 19, 2006, event included Jesse McCartney, all of the other *High School Musical* stars, teen pop sensation JoJo, Lewis Black, and, of course, Santa Claus, who even posed for a picture with Corbin.

To benefit the Fifth Annual Clothes Off Our Back Emmy auction, Corbin donated the bright yellow T-shirt that he wore to the 2006 Teen Choice Awards, at which *High School Musical* won for the best comedy on TV. The money raised from the auction benefits children's charities. Corbin's T-shirt, which was a size small and was autographed by the actor, raised an amazing $320.

There are frequent Clothes Off Our Back auctions. The organization was started by Jane Kaczmarek, best known for playing the harried mom on *Malcolm in the Middle*, and her husband, *Studio 60 on the Sunset Strip* star Bradley Whitford.

The couple wanted to help children's and emergency relief charities, and they thought a great way to do so would be by getting celebrities to donate clothes and other personal items for auction. Since the organization was founded in 2002, more than $1 million has been raised for a number of charities. And almost five hundred celebrities have donated items to the causes.

Corbin seems to love working with children. He took part in the 14th Annual Camp Ronald McDonald Halloween Carnival, which was held on the back lot of Universal Studios in Universal City, California, on October 22, 2006. It was a day of fun and games for children suffering from terminal diseases. Other celebrities at the carnival included Johnny Pacar, Chris Massey, Lauren Storm, Monique Coleman, Ben Stiller, *American Idol*'s Randy Jackson, and Taylor Lautner.

One of the most inspiring organizations that

Corbin volunteers his time and celebrity for is the Starlight Starbright Children's Foundation. The foundation was founded by the famous movie director Steven Spielberg. It was created to help sick kids and their families when a child is suffering from a disease.

The organization builds playrooms in hospitals, connects sick kids to one another and to the rest of the world, and helps kids with terminal illnesses feel normal again. It also sponsors events for families in order to escape the depression and sadness that can come from having a sick child.

Those events can include mother-daughter makeovers, cruises, circus trips, and more. In short, the Starlight Starbright Children's Foundation helps to instill hope where there might not be much reason for hope. The organization helps more than two million children every single year.

Corbin is a member of the Starlight Starbright Children's Foundation Star Power group, a group of teenagers that includes actors, musicians, athletes, artists, and teenage community leaders.

The teens in the Star Power group are chosen for their leadership and strength, and have committed to help achieve the foundation's goals. Some of them might visit sick kids in the hospital. Others might chat with teens in the foundation's special chat room.

The Star Power members might help organize community events to raise money for Starlight Starbright, or to help raise awareness about the organization. They may also host special Starlight Starbright outings, known as "Great Escapes," which allow the families of sick children to mingle and have a good time.

Corbin is part of the first-ever group of Star Power ambassadors, who were chosen in March 2006. He and the other teens in the group are led by their "fairy godmother," Jamie Lee Curtis, an actress and longtime supporter of the Foundation.

Along with Corbin, the other teens in the first-ever Star Power program are: Charlie Burg, the announcer for *A Stellar Night*; Michelle Flude, a Starlight Starbright child who is a leader in her community; musician Kristy Frank; sports star Morgan Henderson; *Zoey 101*'s Christopher Massey; Chris's brother, Kyle Massey, an actor on *That's So Raven*; Rob Pinkston, who's on *Punk'd* and *Ned's Declassified School Survival Guide*; CJ Sanders, who played the young Ray Charles in the movie *Ray*; Lindsay Shaw, from *Ned's Declassified School Survival Guide*; Corbin's *Flight 29 Down* costar, Lindsay Storm; *The Suite Life of Zack & Cody* and *High School Musical*'s Ashley Tisdale; and Devon Werkheiser, who stars in *Ned's Declassified School Survival Guide*.

Corbin's among a very talented group as part of the Star Power program. But it isn't about hanging out with his friends—though he is lucky to have a few friends in the group. He loves volunteering and thinks it's really important to help other people when you can.

He told the Disney All-Stars that his favorite part of volunteering is "when the kids say, 'Thank you for coming,' and you see their smiling faces, and you can see that we just made their day. . . . Knowing that I did something to help them feel important."

The nice thing is, Corbin would probably volunteer his time and talents even if he wasn't a famous star. He's incredibly aware of the impact that sharing just a little time, or a helping hand, can have.

As he told the Disney All-Stars, "There are so many ways to help your community—even little things, like if you see trash on the ground, pick it up, recycle it. Pretty much anything you enjoy doing—if it's hanging out with kids, if it's working with animals—go to a facility that holds animals, or shelters kids, and just ask to volunteer. If every person did what they could to help, it would be amazing what we could accomplish."

Just look at what Corbin has accomplished. It doesn't take a movie star to help someone less fortunate enjoy a Christmas dinner, or forget for just a while that they have a disease. It doesn't take a movie star to help. It just takes someone with a good heart.

Chapter 13

What's Next?

A TV show. Two Disney movies. An album. A live tour. Not to mention graduating from high school, hanging out with three younger sisters, and managing to have a healthy social life! Corbin has done so much in the last few years, you'd think he'd want to take a break. But that's just not like him! He loves working, and he'll keep on doing it for quite a while.

Corbin does have big college plans, though. He told his online journal at corbinbleu.com that after his high school graduation, he was accepted to Pitzer College in Claremont, California. Pitzer College is a small liberal arts school that prides itself on academic excellence, social responsibility, and diversity. Sounds a lot like Corbin, doesn't it?

Corbin intends to keep on acting and performing, but while he's at college, he'll buckle down and hit the books hard. He's really interested in the social sciences, especially psychology. It makes sense that someone who has worked with so many different people would want to understand how humans work.

Since Corbin's true love is acting, he wants to study something that will help his future career, and psychology would be great for that. Studying psychology could help him understand how to play a wide variety of roles, and inspire him. It would be a great major for someone who's interested in acting, even if that someone wasn't already an established actor!

Corbin told a live chat at teenmusic.com, "I'm actually very interested in psychology right now. That is one thing that I've been into . . . hopefully going to major in college. I used to actually want to be a doctor, a pediatrician. Once I found out the amount of time that has to be put into it, especially for school, I gave up that idea. I wouldn't be able to continue what I truly love, which is acting."

Many young actors postpone or even put off college indefinitely. For some, that is the right choice: They don't feel as though they need to get any higher education, at least not the academic kind, when they have already decided that their career will be in the performing arts. And that's fair. After all, if a person has been working for fifteen years, as many college-aged actors have been, why bother stopping a career for four years to get a degree?

But other young performers, like Corbin, see it another way. Even though he plans to continue to work in the entertainment industry when he is an adult, Corbin feels that it is important for him to go to college. He told teentelevision.com, "It's always good to continue to educate yourself. I definitely want to do that." And he's right: Education isn't just about getting a job and making more money. It's about filling up your mind with more information, more understanding.

And of course, college isn't just about education! It's also about experience. Corbin was only in a regular high school for a year and a half, and spent the rest of the time either homeschooled or being tutored on a television or movie set. He's had to act like an adult for much of his life, managing a career and behaving professionally. Of course, Corbin is not the kind of guy who will ever behave unprofessionally. But he is probably looking forward to spending some time surrounded by his peers.

If his experience on *Flight 29 Down* tells us anything, it's that Corbin has a great time when he's around a bunch of people his age. Sure, he can get along with adults—they all seem to respect him a lot. But he thrives on the company of like-minded and similarly aged people. And college will be a great time for him to be able to spend time with people his age.

Ideally, Corbin would like to go to a college that will also allow him to work in theater while studying. He talked about applying to some schools in New York City and in Los Angeles because of their close proximity to thriving theater communities.

But, as he told Celeb101.com, he doesn't want to use his college education as a time to take more acting classes. After all, he's been working since he was two. He said, "I've been acting my whole life, I attended arts high school, and I've done plenty of schooling for my craft. Plus I really feel like psychology will connect into what I already do—the study of the human mind is fascinating to me."

Once he has graduated from college, Corbin will absolutely keep acting and performing. He told a live chat at teenmusic.com, "It is one of those things that when you get up in the morning, that is what you want to do. No matter what, any time of the day, I can act. I can dive into a character and I feel at home. It is who I am."

In a way, college will be a meaningful challenge for Corbin. He isn't often nervous when he's acting, because he's been doing it so long. And he's very, very used to performing in front of an audience. He may not be so used to writing research papers. He may not be used to giving presentations and taking final exams.

Corbin is the kind of person who craves new challenges. Here's hoping that whatever he decides to do in regards to college is the right choice for him—we bet we'll be hearing more about his plans over the next few years!

After college, Corbin will most likely return to acting . . . and singing, and dancing. After all, he has too many talents to not return to some sort of performing! When KriSeLen.com asked where Corbin saw himself five years from now, Corbin replied, "Hopefully having continued success in my career. I would like to be well known for my skills as an actor and work with some of my role models such as Johnny Depp and Denzel Washington. I would mainly like to have the control to put together my own projects. Also, I love to travel, so I hope to continue to get roles that give me that opportunity."

But no matter what, he wants to continue to work. Corbin will never be the kind of guy who just disappears from the world. Success and being respected is really important to him—and, of course, he loves performing.

Corbin is incredibly driven. He wants to be successful. He wants to be respected. He told thestarscoop.com, "I want to achieve success in a way that is not necessarily that I have to do films as much as that I want to achieve success that people know my work and they know that my work is appreciated. [For example], to me, winning an Oscar is a big deal, because it's that your work is known, and put a lot into it. Not the red carpet, but the actual winning. That's what it's all about, the work."

Chapter 14

A Day in Corbin's Life

The first thing Corbin does every morning is hit the snooze button on his alarm clock. Like most teenage boys (and girls, too), he loves to sleep in! Of course, sometimes that's not possible—he might have a call time to be on set for a movie or TV show as early as 5:30 A.M. And he says it takes him a while to get ready in the morning, so he has to factor that time in.

After he's showered and dressed, he has to take care of that famous head of hair of his. On his online journal at corbinbleu.com, he gave these hair tips, steps to achieve the perfect Corbin curls:

* Wash
* Condition
* Comb through with a wide-tooth comb while conditioner is still in
* Rinse

❋ Bend over and shake (this will look something like a wet dog)
❋ While still wet, gently (to not disturb the curls) apply a small amount of anti-frizz cream
❋ Bend over and shake again (try not to get a headache)
❋ Voilà! One crazy head of curls!

Once his hair is done, he's ready to get moving.

He's not a huge fan of cereal for breakfast, so if there's time, Corbin loves to have a big, delicious plate of pancakes in the morning.

Then he's off. First stop? Coffee Bean, the Los Angeles coffeehouse, where Corbin picks up a spicy and sweet chai latte, made of chai tea and hot, steamed milk. Luckily for Corbin, there are more than one hundred and fifty Coffee Bean locations within one hundred miles of Los Angeles—meaning that he can get his favorite drink no matter where he is!

Once he gets to the set, the studio, or to that morning's volunteer location, Corbin's all business. That doesn't mean he doesn't have fun on the set, though! He loves his costars on *Flight 29 Down*, gets along great with the *High School Musical* costars, and has a ton of respect for the producers working with him on his album.

Corbin's MO isn't to get the job done as fast as possible and get out of there. While he does everything with extreme professionalism, he also likes to mix business with pleasure. He loves to work, and he wants to share that love with the other people working with him. It's more fun that way.

For lunch, it's a quick drive over to In-N-Out Burger, the famous West Coast drive-through burger chain. Corbin loves his burgers and fries, and he always gets a double-double burger with grilled onions—animal style—along with fries and a lemonade. Don't know the lingo? Corbin's order will show up with a burger with two patties and two slices of American cheese, lettuce, tomato, and onions. Because he gets it "animal style," the restaurant will grill his onions, add a pickle and extra In-N-Out spread, and the meat will be mustard-cooked. Yum! Yeah, it's junk food. But Corbin stays in shape by working out and dancing, activities that burn calories and fat.

After lunch it's back to work. Once the workday is over—and some days, when there's tons of filming to be done, it isn't over till late—Corbin wants to relax. Corbin also works out every day—exercising after work is a great way to let off steam.

His mom usually makes dinner for him, if he's eating at home that night. He's pretty adventurous with food, but the one thing he really doesn't like is curry. He does like sushi and, of course, hamburgers!

After dinner, if he's up for hanging out, he might use his Treo to call his friends. He might hang out with his friends at The Grove in Los Angeles. Or they might take in a show, go ice-skating, or hang out at a bowling alley. If he's feeling more like a homebody, he might watch some DVDs in his basement, or play with his three younger sisters. If he feels like being alone, he might play the piano for a while. But the ultimate night out for Corbin? He told MissOandFriends.com that it would be "dancing the night away."

Once he's home after a fun evening, it's time for bed. After all, he's going to get up the next day and do it all over again. Luckily for Corbin, he's having fun and making friends the entire time. Corbin is lucky to have found a career that he's good at and that makes him incredibly happy.

Chapter 15
Corbin's Acting Advice

f, like Corbin, you have a deep love for all things acting, that's fantastic! Being an actor and performer has been a great career for Corbin—he loves what he does, and he'd probably want to hear that other people love acting, too.

But it doesn't come easily. Being a successful actor takes a lot of time and patience. It is easy to become discouraged if an audition doesn't result in a callback or if you flub a line onstage. Many people have tried their hand at acting only to become disillusioned with the process.

The first step is to take a good look at your expectations. If you've been in a couple of movies and starred on a television show, like Corbin did before he was cast in *High School Musical*, then it might not be out of line to assume that you, too, can land a plum role in the next Disney hit. But most of us have to be a little bit more reasonable!

Start out by checking out classes in your area. If your school doesn't offer any acting classes or extracurricular activities that involve acting, you can try talking to a teacher or counselor to see if you can start up a club for other aspiring thespians (that's the cool word for actors!).

You can also try to find a community theater in your town. Many community theater groups hold open auditions, meaning anyone can try out for a part in an upcoming production. Find out what plays are up next, and see if there's a part for you! If there is, find out what the requirements for auditions are.

Sometimes actors trying out for a part are asked to memorize a monologue (that's a short speech performed by one person) or to prepare a song. Whatever it is you're asked to do, if you need help, don't be afraid to ask! The Internet is also a great resource for audition help—but be sure to check with a parent before logging on. Your mom or dad can help you find a good site for monologues appropriate to your age and for the play you're trying out for. There are also lots of books that contain audition-ready monologues.

Another place to check for acting opportunities is a local college. Colleges are full of, well, college-age people. So what are they supposed to do when a play calls for a younger person? They might just need you! Some colleges also offer acting classes that community members can participate in. If a college near you does, check it out! Maybe you have a friend or two who'd be interested, too.

Acting classes are pretty important for young actors just starting out. You will learn how to improvise, how to move your body, and get help with lending emotional weight to a scene. Lots of current stars have taken acting classes. Even Corbin—who started acting when he was two—studied theater in school!

If you can't find any acting classes or opportunities in your area, or if you audition for a play and don't get a part, don't despair. Lots of people you see on television and movies didn't get the first few parts they tried out for. You can easily practice at home—and if you're serious about acting, you will!

It's easy. Find a book or even a magazine article. Stand in front of the mirror and just start reading aloud!

Pay attention to how the words sound. You could even videotape yourself and play it back later for an easy self-critique.

Corbin's long career in acting has made him sort of an expert. Here's some of his advice.

LISTEN

Corbin told KriSeLen.com that listening, and being able to take other people's criticism, was the most important part of his job. He said, "Listen. Always listen. Everyone and everything always has something to offer. Listen to it. Absorb it. Apply it. The entertainment industry is a learning process, and you have to take advantage of each opportunity."

DON'T GIVE UP

It takes a while to get established in any career. The beginning of any new endeavor can be a frustrating time, especially if you expect perfect results right from the start. Be patient with yourself. Corbin told *Family Screen Scene* what he'd like to tell all young actors: "Keep trying. Keep pushing. Don't give up."

STUDY

No one can master a new art immediately. Corbin thinks it's important to always keep learning about what you're interested in. When he was asked, in a live chat on teenmusic.com, for acting tips, he said, "I myself have a big theater background. Theater is a great way to get yourself more accustomed, more used to it. It is pretty much the root of acting, I would say. It is raw, everything is raw, what you do. Study. You've got to continue to always grow with your art."

STAY HUMBLE

Even once you have achieved success, it's important to remember that there will always be someone more talented, or better-looking, or funnier than you. That's true of every single career. Corbin told thestarscoop.com, "You have to remember that this is a job; it's not this whole other entity that they try to make it all about being a celebrity. Remember there are people struggling in this world, and you're just lucky enough to be able to get what you have. Stay humble, and remember that it's your job. Accept it graciously, and don't make a big deal of it."

BELIEVE IN YOURSELF

The core of Corbin's strength? It's knowing that he can do whatever he puts his mind to. Sometimes things take more work than other times. But with perseverance, he can achieve anything. He told *Time for Kids*, "I want my fans to see that the success I've achieved is possible. Whatever they set their minds to, they can go out and do."

REMEMBER YOUR FANS!

When someone is as famous as Corbin, it may be easy to just forget about all of his fans. But Corbin never will. He's infinitely grateful to his fans—he always remembers that they are the reason he's gotten to the place he is. He told KriSeLen.com that he wanted to send a message to his fans. He said, "Thank you so much for all of your love and support. I really do appreciate it. And always remember that you can achieve whatever you put your mind to. God bless."

Chapter 16

The ancient science of astrology has been used for centuries to parse out what a person's personality is, based on the day they were born. Many people believe that a star sign can indicate many things about a person.

Since his birthday is February 21, Corbin is a Pisces.

In the astrological calendar, Pisces is the last sign. It is a sign associated with human emotions. Pisces are believed to be kind, emotional, dreamy people. They are honest and generous, but they can sometimes be oversensitive. Pisces is a great sign for an actor to have, because a person born under Pisces understands the full range of human emotions—because they experience them so frequently.

But don't mistake a Pisces for a softy. These

people are fiercely passionate about things they care about. That's another good quality for an actor to have. Though at times Pisces can be withdrawn and self-indulgent, it's usually because they're just taking care of themselves. They have a highly sensitive radar to when they need some pampering.

People who were born under the sign of Pisces are among the friendliest people. They tend to draw other people to them—sounds like our Corbin, doesn't it? They are also very creative and thirst for further knowledge. Perhaps that explains why Corbin wants to go to college even though he has a career already in place—his Pisces nature just won't let him stop learning!

Pisces is one of the three water signs. Like Cancer and Scorpio, Pisces are incredibly intuitive and emotional. Water, a free-flowing but containable element, describes how Pisces are: It is always moving and changing, but controlled. Water signs respond to gut feelings, and it shows in Corbin's career moves that he has responded to an instinct telling him what roles to take on next.

Pisces can be workaholics, so that's something Corbin might want to pay attention to. If he finds that he's not taking care of his personal and social lives, he may want to cut back on the working a little bit. He'll need to pay attention to that in college as well, and be sure to carefully manage his time and not overbook himself with too many activities on top of schoolwork and friends.

Sometimes, Pisces can also be scatterbrains. It doesn't seem like Corbin has that trait—he's far too driven and focused. But it might be something he'll need to watch in the future. If he finds himself overwhelmed by too much happening in his life, an easy fix would just be to cut out some of the stress.

Another personality trait that Pisces are known for is their commitment to taking care of others. That trait shows itself in Corbin's vast body of volunteer work. Pisces can be self-centered at times, but they can also be incredibly generous to others, and at their best are known for putting others ahead of themselves. If Corbin weren't already an actor, he might consider becoming a therapist, a doctor, or a veterinarian.

Pisces can be incredible artists. Corbin is lucky to have found a number of outlets for being artistic, including dancing, playing the piano, and singing, as well as, of course, acting. Pisces love to express themselves, and since they're so in tune with the spectrum of human emotions, they make wonderful actors who can be sympathetic to many feelings.

Pisces are said to be most compatible with the other water signs, Scorpio and Cancer, because their emotional nature will be mutually understood. But that doesn't mean Corbin won't end up with, say, a fire sign. There are other factors that influence astrological compatibility, like, for example, what time each person in the couple was born. So don't despair if you're not a water sign!

Because Pisces are water signs, they tend to crave living near large bodies of water. And Corbin has always lived near the ocean, both in Brooklyn and Los Angeles. He probably won't be headed to any area that's not on a coast anytime soon.

Other famous Pisces include the scientist Albert Einstein, the writers Anaïs Nin, John Irving, John Updike, and W. H. Auden, the famous film director Robert Altman, Chelsea Clinton, and the actors Kristin Davis, Peter Fonda, and Dakota Fanning.

Chapter 17

Corbin by the Numbers

NUMEROLOGY CHART

1	2	3	4	5	6	7	8	9
A	B	C	D	E	F	G	H	I
J	K	L	M	N	O	P	Q	R
S	T	U	V	W	X	Y	Z	

Another way to discover a star's hidden personality can be by using numerology. Numerology, like astrology, is an ancient science that has been used by mathematicians since the time of the Greek philosopher Pythagoras. While it's not as respected as, say, biology, many people turn to numerology to help them understand themselves, others, or situations.

To find a person's numerological number, each letter in their name is assigned to a corresponding number. For example, Corbin equals $3 + 6 + 9 + 2 + 9 + 5 = 34$.

Then the digits are added, so 3 + 4 = 7. His full name is Corbin Bleu Reivers, which adds up to 89. Add 8 + 9 to get 17, and then, finally, 1 + 7 to receive Corbin's number, which is 8.

That might be luckier than Corbin even knows. Eight is the number of prosperity and success in many different numerological systems, including the ancient Chinese system. It can also stand for power and sacrifice. Eights have natural leadership and are able to accumulate lots of money—sounds pretty great, right?

If Corbin weren't such a great guy, being an eight might cause him to be greedy. But we already know that he's not a selfish or greedy person. Because he is so giving, he will always continue to gain power and success and wealth, but instead of using that power selfishly, he will use it for the benefit of others.

Eights are also great judges of character. Corbin seeks out friends who complement him, not the kind of people who would judge him or use him. That's an important thing for an actor to do, especially a young one. Many people might want to be friends with Corbin simply because he is famous, but Corbin knows better than to associate with those people. He wants true, real friends. That's the same instinct that tells him that honesty is the most important quality of a healthy relationship.

Eights can be religious, and Corbin is certainly aware of that part of his personality. He signs off of each of his entries on his online journal with a Bible quote. He respects and is careful of others' religions, however.

Eights are dependable, practical, and good at running businesses—perfect qualities to have, should Corbin decide to become a film producer. He'll need to be able to manage not just the artistic aspects of filmmaking, but the practical ones as well, balancing budgets and keeping things on schedule. Since he's an eight, that should be pretty easy for him.

Of course, it is Corbin himself who has strengthened all of these good qualities. Numerology is just an interesting way to look at the forces that might be behind him, helping him along the way.

Chapter 18

Take the Corbin Quiz!

So, you think you know Corbin pretty well, huh? Take this quiz and see how much you really know!

1. How many sisters does Corbin have?

2. What is Corbin's birthday?

3. Where was Corbin born?

4. What's the name of the first modeling agency Corbin signed with?

5. What's Corbin's character's name on *Flight 29 Down*?

6. What's Corbin's favorite food?

7. What play did Corbin perform in as his first professional acting job?

8. What is Corbin's zodiac sign?

9. What's the name of Corbin's character in *High School Musical*?

10. What's Corbin's dad's name?

11. What does Corbin want to major in during college?

12. Who is Corbin's favorite musician?

13. Where did Corbin's mom go to high school?

14. Who were Corbin's costars in *Catch That Kid*?

15. How old was Corbin when he began working?

16. What's the name of the high school in *High School Musical*?

17. What is Corbin's lucky charm?

18. What role did Corbin initially audition for in
    High School Musical?

19. What was the first show Corbin was on?

20. What color are Corbin's eyes?

Chapter 19

Internet Resources

So many exciting things have taken place for Corbin in the last couple of years that it's hard to keep track of them all, so we've made it simpler for you. To keep up on the latest news about Corbin Bleu, see red-carpet photographs, and read reviews about his movies, bookmark these Internet sites and check back to find out what he's up to! (Don't forget to get permission from your parents before you go online—and remember, some websites disappear, and new ones pop up every day!)

Corbin's official website
www.corbinbleu.com

Corbin on the Internet Movie Database
imdb.com/name/nm0088298

Corbin's MySpace page
www.myspace.com/corbinbleu

Discovery site for *Flight 29 Down*
www.flight29down.com

Corbin on TV.com
www.tv.com/corbin-bleu/person/34256/summary.html

Volunteering is really important to Corbin. To learn
more about Corbin's volunteer work, go to
www.starlightstarbright.org
disney.go.com/allstars

To get involved in a volunteering program of your
own, talk to your school's counselor or visit the website
www.volunteermatch.org. (Please make sure to talk to
your parents before signing up for any volunteer work.)

Chapter 20
Just the Beginning

Obviously, Corbin Bleu isn't your average young actor. He's got a lot of heart and soul. But one of the things Corbin is most admired for is his fearlessness. A lot of teenage guys might be embarrassed to admit that they love dancing, musicals, and playing the piano. But not Corbin. He is unabashed about everything he does—and his talents are stronger because of it. He's not just a cute, young actor. He's a cute, young, *talented* actor.

We expect to see a lot more come from this multitalented young star. He might take a few years off for college, but then he'll be back, with even more tricks up his sleeve! Whether it's producing, directing, dancing, singing, or acting, Corbin Bleu will continue to push it to the limit—and he'll take us with him on his wild ride!